A Hungarian Woman's Life

Erzsebet Kertesz Dobosi Croll

Eloquent Books
New York, New York

Designed by Donald L. Croll and Erzsebet K. Croll

Eloquent Books
An imprint of AEG Publishing Group
845 Third Avenue, 6th Floor - 6016
New York, NY 10022
www.eloquentbooks.com

ISBN: 978-1-60860-437-1

Printed in the United States of America

Book Design: Stacie Tingen

Photo Credit—the cover photo is from my collection. It was taken shortly after I arrived as a refugee at the Dominion Gardens apartment complex in Alexandria, Virginia.

I am wearing a much-appreciated dress donated to me by a charity in U.S. Army Camp Kilmer, New Jersey, in route to Virginia.

To my loving husband, Dr. Donald L. Croll, who supported me in writing this book and helped me translate the book from Magyar (Hungarian) to English.

To my good friend, Barbara Lightner, who encouraged me to write this book and helped me to get started.

Contents

My Life's Miracles

Chapter 1

1940: Peace

On a beautiful April morning in 1940, Mother got our family a baked Easter ham, sausage, and hard boiled eggs that were painted red and placed in a basket. I remember how beautiful they looked in the basket with the white cloth. Mother said she was taking all the food to the church so the priest could bless it and then she would hurry home so we could have it for lunch. I have to tell you how excited we were. The three of us looked out the window as Mother left. Snow covered the ground. Big icicles were hanging from the gutter. In the meanwhile, Uncle Steve arrived. He was my mother's younger brother. We were very happy to see him. He always brought us writing paper, erasers, pencils, and little blackboards. The rest of the relatives came.

Mother returned from the church. The table was beautifully set with white table cloth and holiday china on it. The fire was burning in the fireplace. Julie was sitting in her playpen and the three of us were sitting at the table next to the grownups. I remember how it was a very special holiday. That's how Easter was celebrated in our house.

Finally, it was summer. We could to go outside to play. I talked my twin sister into throwing rocks up to the roof to see who could throw them the furthest. Of course, we were only five years old. My rock landed in the middle of the big picture window. Wow! *That will be big trouble*, I thought. I ran right into the house to tell Mother that Anna's rock went through the window.

She was right at my heel, yelling, "It's not true! Mother, it's not true!"

My poor mother didn't know what to do. She said, "Just wait until your father gets home."

1

Well, I thought, *that's the time he usually gets home. I had better go to bed and act like I am sleeping. I am sure he is not going to wake me up to spank me.* The window got fixed. I got away without being spanked.

It looked like we are going to have a new baby. In May 1942, the stork arrived. He brought us a little girl—Maria. Now there were five of us, one boy and four girls.

Father was working for the government. October 1942, after dinner, Father said he had big news. We were going to move. He got a new job. Mother wasn't happy for the news. That meant we were not going to be seeing the relatives, because we would live in a new city that was quite far away.

The time came when Father had to take over the new job. Mother dressed us very warmly since it was October and very cold in Transylvania. My uncle took us to the train station. Wow! When I saw that train for the first time in my life, I was only six years old. I was amazed that something like that was in existence. Right away, I fell in love with it. Goodbyes were said. We sat down in the cabin. It had big, beautiful, comfortable seats, and it was nice and warm. I thought, *It is not just beautiful outside, but inside, too.* When it started to pull out of the train station, the sound was unbelievably strong.

From the cabin window, we watched the Transylvanian forest. I said to Ann, "We should count them. See how many trees there are." But the excitement of the day got us tired. We decided the train was going too fast for us to count the many trees. We put ourselves in a comfortable position.

Right away, a new miracle happened. We never saw such darkness in our whole life. It was darker than dark. Of course, we started crying because we couldn't see our parents. I thought, *Why is that train running so fast into the darkness? Probably, it is going to fall straight down a ravine.*

By the time I was finished with that thought, we looked at our parents, shocked. They explained to us that it was a tunnel and nothing to worry about. We really didn't understand the whole thing, but we hoped there wouldn't be any more tunnels. But, there were several more. We were very happy every time there was light again.

In the early afternoon, we arrived at the town of Oradna. Mr. Varga was waiting for us with a big snow sled. We were twenty kilometers from our new home. The train only came that far. Beautiful red horses pulled the snow sled. An oil coach lantern hung next to Mr. Varga. I was wondering why he needed that lamp. Pretty soon, it got dark and the lamp gave light, and the wolves were afraid of that sort of light. The Transylvanian forest had a lot of wolves in it. I hoped Mr. Varga was prepared for them. The two beautiful horses traveled in the quiet, snow-covered forest. Only the snow sled runners broke the quiet of that snow-covered forest. To me, the forest covered with snow was like a story book world. Finally, we arrived at Lajosfalva, our new home. Of course, we didn't see much of it because it was dark.

But in the morning, we awoke and we very much wanted to know where we had come to. Father went to take over his new job. Mother took the three of us to sign us in at the school. John went to the second grade, and Anna and I were in the first grade. I remember we had a pretty lady teacher. During the day, we found the river, not too far behind our house. The name of it was Aranyosbeszterce. We said we were going to swim there in the summer.

This was not a bad place we had moved to! From our house, not too far, was a big bridge. On that bridge, you were able to go to Romania. There were Hungarian soldiers guarding the Hungarian side. On the Romanian side, there were Romanian soldiers on guard..

One day in the summer of 1942, we went swimming in the river. That was wonderful! You can't ask for anything better than that. Here, all of the town's children enjoyed the swimming immensely. Only Mother was sad, as she missed the relatives.

In January 1944, we got a new baby. Her name was Rozsa. Mother was getting used to our new home. We had good neighbors. School was going well. The priest had heard that Mother baked very delicious bread. He asked her if she would be kind enough to bake his bread, too. She said she would be glad to. That went on until the priest beat John because he didn't know the homework. John ran home from school. His shirt was bloody. As soon as Mother found out what happened, she went and beat up the priest. The priest was so much ashamed of himself that he decided not to report Mother to the authorities.

Chapter 2

1944: War Came

One day in August, we were standing on the sidewalk in front of our neighbor's house. Mother and the other grownups were crying. Mr. Rosenberg and Mrs. Rosenberg's coats had a big, yellow star. They were speaking very quietly. For an eight-year-old child, it was hard to understand what is going on. One thing was sure; those yellow stars mean something very bad.

By September 1944, it looked like war had come to our little town, too. The postman brought my father's draft notice. In two weeks, he had to go to war. A couple of days after the notice, we heard a lot of noise in our street. We were thinking maybe the circus is coming to town. The loudspeaker was informing the town's people that we had twenty-four hours to leave the town. If not, everyone would be severely punished. The town's men called a meeting. They tried to decide where to go. Oradna was the nearest city, where Mr. Varga had been waiting for us with the sled in October 1942. The townspeople decided they were going to form a caravan. Everyone had a wagon and horses. That way, everybody would be able to leave the town.

The town's people got ready. Only the most necessary items were taken, since everyone had three or four children who needed space on the wagons. Half way to our destination, Mrs. Kovacs' wagon wheel broke. My father needed to make room for Mrs. Kovacs and her daughter, Mariskanak. This wasn't easy because there were already six children, Mother and Father, and our belongings. Some of our things would need to be left behind. The children were taken off of the wagon and some of the clothes removed to make space for the Kovacs.

In Transylvania, the forest was very, very cold, and our baby, Rozsa, caught pneumonia. We were going very slowly because the road already

5

had land mines planted. Mother was very ill, too. Three days before our departure, she had very painful arthritis in both legs and she was screaming in pain. Therefore, she wasn't able to help Father. Finally, we got to our destination.

Poor little Rozsa got sicker. There were people trying to medicate Mother. There were no doctors anywhere. The ten-month-old Rozsa was very sick.

Mother was in excruciating pain. She yelled loudly because of the pain. We couldn't go into her room. As I passed by the door one day, to my amazement, I saw Mother lying on her stomach. Both her legs were covered with leaches, black and very fat. When they filled up with blood, then they were taken off her legs. That was a very scary sight for me. They said the leaches were going to take out the bad blood and her pain was going to get better. We had no doctor. We needed a doctor and penicillin.

Mrs. Parc came to the house. She had with her about two yards of beautiful, pink silk material. She wanted to sell it to my mother. She said, "You can make some dresses for the girls."

We thought it was beautiful. Rozsa was standing in her crib. She was looking at the beautiful material laid out. Rozsa got hold of it and pulled it to herself. Mother said, "Look at her. She wants it for herself." Mother bought the material and she said, "We will decide later what we are going to make out of this material."

There was a lot of commotion on the street. We ran out to see what was going on. In the middle of the road, captured Romanian soldiers were being marched by German soldiers. By that time, everybody was standing out on the sidewalk. That was the first time we had seen so many soldiers. The women were throwing bread at the prisoner soldiers. When the prisoners bent down to pick the bread up, the German soldiers beat them with a whip. Even today, when I think of it, my throat gets tight and my tears come into my eyes. Now we were starting to understand the yellow stars on our neighbors' clothes, and why we had to leave our home. Poor little Rozsa is still very sick and Mother feels somewhat better

Chapter 3

September 1944: Little Rozsa Died

We awoke to a very sad morning. Mother was crying. She told us that poor little Rozsa died. We looked at her. She looked like she was sleeping, except that she was very pale.

Mother asked us if we remembered the pink silk material she bought from Mrs. Parc. We said, "Yes, we remember."

Mother said, "That's going to be Rozsa's burial dress." She dressed up an eleven-month-old baby. There was enough material to make a cover for the tiny, little casket. Father found a priest and, with the neighbors, they went to the cemetery to bury poor little Rozsa. She was the first victim of the war. We were not able to go because the cemetery was too far.

Father heard that in Romania there was a Romanian arthritis doctor. It would be nice if he would look at my mother because she was still suffering very much. They left the house. We were told to watch out for the little ones. That was a big responsibility. At the time, Julia was only five years old, Maria was two, and John, ten. He was never there, anyway, therefore, Ann and I watched over the little ones.

The weather was very pleasant. There was no school. There was a war going on. We were outside a lot and playing. In the neighbor's yard, there was a very big pear tree which had those little, sweet pears on it. It wasn't much food; therefore, we ate from the tree a lot of times.

Finally, Mother and Father got home from the doctor. They told us that Mother got medicine and they had other big news for us. Mother was pregnant. I remember we weren't too happy for the news. Father got a letter that we should get ready because we were getting a train wagon. The government was taking us to a safer place. Father said that he would go back to our hometown and see if he could bring at least some of our clothes back with him. Mother told him to be very careful and please hurry back.

Two days later, my father came home empty-handed. We asked him, "Where are our clothes?"

He said the house was taken over by German soldiers. The soldiers wouldn't allow him to take anything out of the house. He said, "I told them, 'That is my house! The children need their clothes', but they still didn't allow me to have anything."

Therefore, he came back empty-handed. We received the train wagon. The government gave one for each family. They gave us Mr. Brown, who was alone. He was a shoemaker. The wagon had been used to transport hogs. It was two levels, and you couldn't stand up in it. Father cut a hole big enough to be able to stand up. And, from outside, the wind blew in, because there were slits in the walls. He located some tarpaper and made a wall, so the wind didn't blow into the wagon.

Father was getting really nervous, since the draft notice was in his pocket. He could not join the military until the family was in a secure place. The news was that those who had the draft notice and were not joining the military, they would find them and hang them. Poor Father, he was really in big trouble.

One day in October 1944, everyone was in the railroad car. Tomorrow we would be leaving. Now we were counted as refugees. We were not sure who we were fleeing from. The train was very long. The only time you could see the end of it was when we were on a curve. It was exciting and, at the same time, a very unsure feeling, since we had no idea of where this train was taking us.

I don't remember what we were eating. When there was a corn field or sunflower field, the train slowed down so the men could jump off of the train to pick corn from the corn field, and they went back up on the train. The train tried to go as slow as it could. We used to tell Father, "Run Father, run. You can make it!" Finally, he would jump on the train with a half sack of corn or sunflowers; whatever was there.

Chapter 4

November 1944: Our First Bombing

In November, we were in Hungary from Transylvania. We were at some big city. There were a lot of railroad tracks, at least twenty-five of them. Our train was standing still. A short time passed and the sirens were wailing. A couple of minutes later, a loud speaker screamed that we would have to go to the bunker because the planes were coming to bomb. Mother was holding Maria, who was two years old. John was holding Julia's hand. Father was holding Anna's and my hand, and we were running. The planes were very loud. It was very, very scary. We fell down many times on the railroad tracks. Finally, we came to some bunkers.

A few hours later, when we came up from the bunkers, the planes had left. It was quiet, and the sun was shining, then we saw our knees and legs were full of blood. The blood had already dried on our legs, because we had fallen down on the railroad tracks.

Father said, "We are missing our train. Someone took it." We could not see it anywhere. He asked the station master if he knew where our train was.

The station master, Mr. Varga, said, "It is here somewhere; you just have to find it. They must have put it on a different track." He was looking for it and looking for it, until he finally located it.

We very gladly crawled back into our place, as we were very, very, tired. It was a very exciting day. I believe that was the first time we had heard airplanes.

A short time passed and Mr. Balog came. He was responsible to make sure everyone was on the train. He said, "We are staying here about a half hour. Over there is a little store and you can buy some bread."

Our dinner was jelly sandwiches. When it was almost dark, the train began moving. Everybody was in their own space. When I woke up, I was cold and I had to pee. It was okay; it was already morning. Mother said we had some bread left over, so that would be our breakfast.

At around noon, the train stopped. We were seeing again a lot of train tracks. We hoped we wouldn't have to run again and that the planes were not coming.

Mr. Balog came and said, "We are staying here about one hour because we don't have a train track to go further. And at the train station, we will be able to buy bread and sausage."

We stayed on the train and Father went to the store. A short time later, he returned with the very fresh bread, sausage, and four apples. Mother cut it up and divided it six ways. We ate that, too. We found out we were in some big city called Debrecen. There were a lot of railroad tracks, military hardware, and tanks. We were wondering where they were going.

Mr. Balog came and said, "We are leaving in one hour."

The people asked, "Are you sure?"

He said, "If God is willing."

In early November 1944, the days were short, and cold, too. One day, we arrived in Demecser, at the railroad station. In between the railroad tracks a lot of soldiers were sitting. Some of them were even crying. They were German prisoners. The Russians were guarding them. In Transylvania, the German soldiers were guarding the Romanian soldiers, and they were beating them when they bent down to pick up the bread the people threw to them. What a change!

Today, we ate very well. The townspeople heard refugees were in the train station. They brought us warm, cooked food like stuffed cabbage. It was different than what my mother made. The meat was mixed with corn meal. It was very good. I can still taste it in my mouth.

Father was very nervous. He told the railroad station master he had a draft notice in his pocket. He had to join the military, but he didn't know what to do with his family—his wife and children. The railroad master told Father there was no where to go, anyway. The war was everywhere, now.

We were in great danger in the train wagon because they were bombing the military transport replacements. The station master was going to talk to the mayor of the city. He should give us a house. There were a lot of empty houses since they took the Jewish people away.

Chapter 5

November 1944: Our New Home in Demecser

The mayor of the town gave us a house. The mayor showed the house to us. It was on the main street. It was a big corner house. It had beds in it, closets, and some other furniture, and a stove. Father said to Mother, "You will be all right here until I get back."

John was somewhere getting to know the neighborhood. Father had to wait for him to come back. When he did, Father spanked him and told him he was the man in the house until he came back, and he had to watch over everything. Now this place is our home. John was only ten years old. It was an awful big responsibility for a little kid like that. Father said his goodbyes to all of us and he promised he would be back as soon as possible.

Of course, Mother cried all night long. She was very much afraid in a strange country and a strange house. In the morning, the neighbors came. They already knew we were refugees from Transylvania. They also knew Father had left last night to join the war. They promised they would be helpful as much as possible. Mother thanked them very much and she asked them where the store was.

We went to the store to buy flour, sugar, potatoes, tea, and oil. Some firewood was in the house. Mother was able to cook supper and tea. The house got a little warmer, too.

The next night in that big house, Mother cried very hard. She was worrying about Father. She was wondering where the people from this house went when they were dragged away. I don't think she slept any that night. She knew this was a Jewish house. She was lucky she didn't know what terrible things were happening to those people.

The third day we were there, there was a very loud noise from the street. Everybody was standing on the sidewalk. We were watching what was happening. Russian soldiers with about twenty horse wagons were taking their wounded soldiers. Among them was a woman soldier. Her bloody hair hung down from the wagon, as she was lying in the bottom of the wagon. I was amazed—a woman soldier! As we were standing there, Mother saw Mrs. Szolem, who had brought the stuffed cabbage for us at the railroad station. She told her she was extremely afraid in that house. Mrs. Szolem said that in her yard there was an empty room. We could move in there if we liked. Maybe it would be better for us. She had about six children, too, and we could play with them. Mother probably wouldn't be so afraid. She thanked Mrs. Szolem. She said, "We will be there this afternoon." I remember it was a long room, separated from the rest of the house. It was in the same yard.

John was going with the neighborhood kids. Shortly after, he came back home with two big pan-sized pieces of potato candy. Mother asked him where he got it. He said, "The people broke into the sugar factory." He was in a hurry and was running back to get a sack of sugar cubes.

The next day, the people broke into the lumber factory. He came and said he needed help because the lumber was too long. Ann and I had to go help him bring it home. Then, we had something to cook with and to heat for winter.

There was an apple orchard, and the owner probably had been taken away. We went and picked the apples and got a big basket full. We picked sunflowers and corn. It looked like we had a lot of stuff to eat until Father got home from the war. Of course, there was no school. The war was going on.

The Russian soldiers came looking for German soldiers. On the bed were big feather covers. The Russian soldier put his sword in it, thinking a German soldier may be hiding in there. Then they came and asked for food. Mrs. Szolem called all of the children together and told the children that when the soldiers come and ask for food, we should all gather and stand in front of them. Mrs. Szolem was a little woman but, boy, could she cry in front of the soldiers! "There is no food to feed the children."

The soldiers said a cuss word and then they left. Mrs. Szolem found out the Russian soldier took her big pot. She really got mad. She said, "Just wait." She said, "I will be right back." Soon after that, she returned with her big pot.

We heard the planes are coming to bomb the city. Everybody should go to the bunkers. Mrs. Szolem's brother had a wine cellar and we went there to be safe. As we were sitting on the floor, there were about twenty of us. A Russian soldier came down and Mariska was sitting in the middle. He got her hand and tried to pull her out. She was about fifteen years old. The women were pulling Mariska's clothes and legs, and were screaming. They were not going to let the soldiers take the young girl out of there. There was a lot of screaming and yelling. The young officer came down to see what was happening. He slapped the soldier's face and told him to go out of there right now. He reassured us not to worry. Nothing was going to happen. It was about midnight when we got home very exhausted. We gladly went to bed.

The next day, children came to town. We were looking at them. They were from Budapest. They were pretty well taken care of. Mrs. Szolem took in two little girls. The neighbors got their little boy about five years old. He did not want to be there. He was crying after his mother. He did all kinds of bad things. He knocked all of the flower pots off of the window sill. He was beating the chickens with a stick. He was lucky he was with very good people.

The parents sent their children to neighboring smaller towns, with government help, trying to protect them from the bombing which Budapest suffered. Can you imagine the emotional stress these parents had when they left their children with complete strangers? But, desperate times require desperate action.

It was almost Christmas in 1944, when Mother found a little Christmas tree, and she baked little, fancy cookies. She also located some walnuts. We decorated the tree with fancy cookies, little apples, and walnuts.

We were very happy to have the Christmas tree, and it was edible. We were sad at the same time, as Father wasn't there, and no one knew where he was. We were thinking back, remembering when we were home in Transylvania, when the angel came and brought the Christmas tree. It was filled with Christmas candy and silver-painted walnuts. We got writing papers, erasers, little blackboards, and fancy pencils.

The doorbell rang. Mother said the angel was coming and we should all kneel down with our hands folded. We right away did what Mother said. She would open the door. There was the angel, with the Christmas tree in her hands. She came in, then the angel said, "Jesus is born." She heard we were good. That is why she brought the Christmas tree, and we would pray for Jesus' coming. It was an unbelievably special Christmas Eve for us little children.

The war had quieted down somewhat, probably because of the Christmas holidays. Mother heated up the room and it was nice and warm. Mrs. Szolem brought delicious stuffed cabbage. From the house where we were before, Mr. Juhasz came, too, and he brought bacon. When Mr. Juhasz left the house, Mother started crying. She was worrying about whether Father had anything to eat.

In 1945, the war was going on. The Germans were in our town, but not for long. The Russians came back and beat them out of the town. In the meanwhile, we had to hide in the bunkers and cellars.

Mother had some phobia problems. She said, "What will happen if the cellar collapses on us?" She decided we were not going to go anywhere. We were going to stay in the house. We went under the beds many times when the planes flew over the town. They were very loud.

One morning in the end of January, we woke up and the town was surrounded with Romanian soldiers. In the houses, the people had to give them shelter and food. We already knew what to do when soldiers asked for food. All ten of us stood in front of them and we looked at them. They said, "My, my, so many children." They knew right away they had to locate food some place else. They left the town after a short while.

In February, Mother bought two geese from Mrs. Toth. Mother said she was going to fatten them up with corn and we were going to have meat and goose lard. She was going to kill one of them as soon as it was fat enough. The other goose would be killed when Father returned from the war.

John found out Mrs. Szapanos was looking for someone who would take out the potatoes from the ground. A big hole was dug in the end of the yard. In the fall, the potatoes were put in the huge hole and covered up with dirt, and that way, they would keep until next spring. John said to Mrs. Szapanos that he had two sisters who could help and we would take out the potatoes, half and half.

She said, "That's a deal! You can start right away."

John came home very excited. He told us what a good deal he had made with Mrs. Szapanos. "We should get a basket and let's go take the potatoes out of the ground."

He pulled the ground off from the potatoes. Right away, you could smell the rotten potatoes. John said to Mrs. Szapanos, "It's all rotten!"

Mrs. Szapanos said, "It has good in it, too!"

We started taking the potatoes out of the pit. Those which were hard went to one pile and the soft ones went to another pile. By the afternoon, we had three baskets of potatoes. Mrs. Szapanos divided them fifty-fifty. We happily took home the potatoes.

Let me tell you how badly the potatoes stink when they are rotten. Even a week later, we were still smelling them.

In March 1945, the Russian soldiers came back to our town, again. They had been here so many times we almost knew how to speak Russian. Mother was feeding the geese. She said in two weeks she would kill one of them. Of course, we were anxiously waiting it. It had been a very long time since we had eaten any kind of meat. And, of course, the goose crackling is very good, too. Just like Mother said, we were not going to the shelter and the cellars. When the planes came, we would hide under the bed. And she pulled the feather comforter on us, so that, if a bomb fell down, it would help to protect us from deafness. We did not know what that meant, but we thought Mother surely knew.

In April 1945, Mother's stomach was getting bigger and bigger. The baby was going to come pretty soon. The war had really quieted down. There were only a few Russian soldiers in the town. Mother was hoping Father would be home pretty soon.

Mother said she was going to kill one of the geese the next day. I don't have to tell you how excited we were. We were anxiously waiting for to-morrow. The day came for the goose to be killed. Mother got a big pot of hot water and sharpened the knife. We went out to get the goose. Mother was looking at them. She said, "Which one should it be?"

John said "That one. It is fatter."

Mother said the other one would get fatter by the time Father got home. That was when we would kill the last one. She cut the goose's neck. The blood was let into a little dish. She fried some onions and the goose blood, and we ate it right away. Mother cleaned the goose. Very carefully, she started cutting it up. She said, "The two legs and the breast, the neck, the back, and the two wings, I will cook soup out of it."

We had a big table. We surrounded it and watched Mother working, cutting the goose up. She said, "Don't stay so close, I might cut you!" We pulled back from the table for a second. We watched, amazed at all that meat.

Mother baked half of the goose, and made some potatoes with it. We were very satisfied with the delicious baked goose.

The parents came from Budapest to get their children. The little boy had been packed for two days. He was suffering terribly without his par-ents. He missed them so very much. The two little girls' parents came, too. They weren't so pretty like when they had first come. The strange place, inadequate food, and their parents' absence was a lot for them. We were looking at the Budapest people. They were skinny and tired looking. They must have had a very hard time in Budapest. Budapest was terribly bombed during the war.

When springtime came, the weather was very pleasant. Spring flowers bloomed in the gardens. The fruit trees were loaded with flowers. In the yards, little chickens, and little ducklings were running around. The hen showed the little chickens how to scratch. The town was filled with fragrance. The men started to come home from the war. The people were saying Mr. Varga had come home from the war. Mr. Toth came home, too.

Those who had sons and husbands in the war went out to the train station, hoping their loved ones would be on the train—the husbands or sons. John went out to the train station every day hoping Father would be on the train, too. He was very sad when he came home to tell Mother he was not on the train. Mother reassured him, "Maybe tomorrow."

Many times, military officials would go to houses to tell the wife or the mother that her loved one didn't make it home, that he had been killed in the war. After that, the poor woman dressed in black. We asked our mother, "Why does Mrs. Kovacs wear black every day?"

Mother explained, "Because her husband died in the war."

So far, we didn't even think it was possible for Father to die in the war. Mother right away reassured us Father didn't die. We were so relieved. John said, "Father better hurry home from the war. That second goose sure is fat."

Mother agreed the goose was really getting fat.

One day, we went to Mr. Varga to help him plant potatoes and sunflowers. In Demecser, they planted a lot of sunflowers. They liked the sunflower oil. They used to put two gallons of oil in a pot. They would put a big slice of bread in it when it was hot, and fry it until it was nice and red. It was very delicious and nourishing, too.

All of our apples were gone. Mother said that, pretty soon, there would be cherries in the farmer's market and we would buy some. After dinner, Mother said we had to kill the goose the next day. It was very fat and she was worried that the goose will die. We all, right away, said, "But Father is not home, yet."

Mother said sadly, "I know, I know."

The next day was Saturday. Mother boiled the water in the pot and sharpened the knife. The little bowl got ready for the goose blood. The goose was cleaned of its feathers. We all said, "My, what a fat goose!"

Mother said, "That goose is going to give a liter of goose lard, for sure."

Of course, we surrounded the table again and we watched how Mother cut up the goose: the two legs, the two wings, the breast.

Chapter 6

Spring 1945: Father Came Home From the War

We heard a knock on the door. Mother stood with her back to the door. She said, "Take a look. Who is it? Who is coming?"

The door opened, and Mr. Toth from next door to the Jewish house, said, "Look, Mrs. Kertesz, who I brought."

Mother turned to the door. Father was standing in the middle of the door! He was skinny and very tired looking. Our happiness was unbelievable. Now, for sure, the war is over. Father had come home for the second goose.

Mother baked the goose in the oven, cooked the soup, and made special noodles for the soup. Our happiness was tremendous. Father was home and the war was over, too! He told stories about what major cities he fought in during the war. We surrounded him, and sat with him all day. The day was filled with tremendous excitement. That night, everyone went to bed willingly. All the excitement just wore us out.

Three days after Father got home from the war, in the early morning, Mother said we needed to get up and get dressed because we had to go over to the neighbor's house. The baby was coming. Mrs. Szolem went to get the midwife. We thought there would be a lot of yelling because, when a new baby came to our house, Mother used to yell loudly. The midwife came. We anxiously waited for our new baby. We started guessing among us whether it would be a boy or a girl. It would be nice to have a boy, since we already had four girls in the family.

About two in the afternoon, Mrs. Szolem came to get us. She told us the baby had come. All of us, at the same time, asked, "What is it?"

She said, "It is a little girl."

We would have been a lot happier if it had been a little boy. She said we could go home and see Mother and the new baby. Mother was tired, but she was well. The neighbor ladies brought dinner. Later on, Mother asked, "What will we name the baby?"

Of course, everyone wanted to give a different name to her. Father said, "We are going to name her Gizi." We looked at each other. "Gizi?" That was a strange name! But that is how Gizi became Gizi.

In the summer of 1945, Father got a letter from the government. Since we were refugees from Transylvania, and we had lost our home because of the war, we would get a house. Father would be able to choose from three counties. The government would move us where ever he chose. Father would have to go pick out the city. He would leave in two days.

Mother told him, "Make sure it is a nice city with good schools and a good opportunity for the children to get educated." She told him he should be very careful and make sure the place would be very nice.

We said goodbye to Father. Two days later, he came back home. Mother asked him, "Did you go to all three counties? You sure came home fast."

His answer was, "We are going to live in a nice town." He would find out the next day when we would move.

In September, we learned that, in two weeks, we would leave for our new home. Mother asked Father, "Tell us, are we going to move to a very nice place?"

Father answered, "Yes, yes!"

Three days before we were to leave, we said goodbyes to our neighbors. They sent their good wishes and they said they would miss us.

Chapter 7

Summer 1945: Our New Home in Szarazd

In the late afternoon, Father said, "We will be there soon." A half hour later, the train stopped at a small train station. Father said, "It is only four kilometers from here to the town we are going to."

There was the man from Transylvania with a horse wagon. There were two big gray horses drawing the wagon. They put our stuff on the wagon, and Father said, "We are going to Szarazd."

Mr. Toth asked "Szarazd?"

Father said, "The house is number 4."

It didn't take long for us to get to Szarazd, since the house was right at the beginning of the town. We were here! We saw a big barn in the yard, a well, and a house right smack across from the barn. The house had one room and a kitchen. When Mother looked down at the floor, all she saw was the ground. She asked Father, "Where is the floor?" She had never seen anything like it—a house without a floor!

Father said, "Maybe that is the style here."

Mother asked, "How many houses are in this town?"

He said, "One hundred and ten."

Poor Mother! She looked like she was going to lose her mind from disappointment. She started to scold him. She asked, "What is wrong with you?"

He had to explain that right away, before Mother lost her mind. He explained that he had gotten drunk on the train and somebody had said that this was a good town. It became clear he had never even seen this town!

Father, lying in the corner, was shaking. He was freezing to death. He was very sick. Maybe he had influenza. We had already covered him up with everything we could, but he was still freezing to death.

Mother ran out to the yard and ran back to the house. She was just scolding Father. She couldn't believe, after so much suffering, that we would wind up in that cheap, little town. I don't remember what we ate for days. Our mother wasn't able to take care of us.

In September 1945, the schools were already in session. Mother said, "Tomorrow we are going to the school to sign up John, Ann, and Erzsebet." The school was in a big house with two large rooms. In one of the rooms, they taught grades one to four. In the other room, they taught grades four to eight. We introduced ourselves to the teacher. John went into the fourth grade. Anne and I went into the second grade, since we lost a year because of the war. The school had about twenty children in each room.

The teacher was of German descent. Soon we found out how much he hated the Hungarian children. A long time ago, the German people were relocated to that town. Our teacher, Mr. Becker, did not like the Hungarians. He was a big man and he hit very hard.

We sat on long benches with a table in front of us; the table had a hole cut out for the ink bottle. When we were writing with ink, the ink bottle was supposed to be in that hole. One day, our session was to write with ink. Behind me, the girl didn't put her bottle in the hole. As I turned, my elbow knocked the bottle over. The ink flowed into the girl's clothes. She started crying. Mr. Becker saw that. He came toward me and he beat me up terribly. He slapped me around. He always physically abused the Hungarian children. He had terrible prejudice towards us. We could hardly wait to get to the other teacher, Mr. Bush. He was of German descent, too. He was a wonderful, kind, teacher. All of the children loved him.

At home, we didn't tell Mother what the Becker teacher was doing. We figured she had enough sorrow.

In 1946, we heard the number 9 house would become vacant. We were thinking it would be nice to move there, since it was a better one than the one we had. Father asked the mayor if it would be okay if we moved in there. He came home very happily. He said, "We are allowed to move in that house." Therefore, we moved into number 9 house. We noticed Mother was pregnant. We were not happy. We were thinking, *Enough of us! Six children should be enough for everybody.*

In 1947, the baby came. Mother said, "She is so beautiful! Maybe it would be okay to name her Rozsa." Since we already had a little baby named Rozsa, who died at the beginning of the war, she worried about that. She had heard it was bad luck and not good to name a new baby after a dead baby.

In 1948, Mr. Bush became our teacher at the school, finally! He never hit us and we got very good grades. We liked him very, very, much.

Papa heard that the main street number 87 house was going to become vacant. He thought it would be nice to move over there. It had two big rooms, a big kitchen, a separate summer kitchen, a big barn for the two horses, and for the cow. It had a big vegetable garden, too. Mother said to Father, "Run to the mayor and ask if we could move into the house.

He came back pretty soon, and said we could move into that nice house the next week. Mother was very happy about it. She whitewashed it and knew how to make a home very pleasant. In that house, finally, everybody had enough room.

In the summer of 1948, political change was in the air. The news was that the German people who were willing to become Hungarian citizens could stay. Otherwise, they were going to be relocated in Germany. There was sadness in the town. It looked like in 1944, when they took the Jewish people away. Mrs. Grundel's daughter was taken away by the Russians, and many others were also taken to work for them. Every parent was hoping their young adult children would come home soon from Russia. When they did come home, how would they find their parents who were not in the town anymore? A few of them stayed, but the rest of them were taken away to Germany. The politics was in progress. Three tired old men—Stalin, Roosevelt, and Churchill—divided Europe up. They should have decided the war was over and everybody should go home. The people suffered tremendously. Hitler was dead. These men didn't care about the people.

Chapter 8

Summer 1948: Communism Takes Over

We wound up with Communism, which caused tremendous suffering and death. We lived in darkness and under terror for the next fifty years.

In 1950, the new Communist regime forced the population into communes. You had to take your belongings into the commune with your horses, cows, and land, to become the property of the commune. At the end of the year, the harvest would be distributed. The people knew this would not work out, but that was the law and the people could not do anything about it. The people were not working the same.

Why do we have wars? The humans can't get along. That is the way humans are. We have to look at the families. I don't know any family who is getting along without jealousy. The humans don't tolerate each other. The problem is when they try to mix the world population.

When the laws are fair in the world, we have leaders who will keep the laws. They look out for the people's interest, then no one has to leave their country—not for political or for economic reasons. God very fairly enriched the world. For example, there are gold, diamonds, oil, gas, coal, good farm land. These could make the population rich, with fair laws and with fair commerce. Every one would live well. There would not be any potbellied children. For example, how many loaves of bread could have been bought with the money Mrs. Marcos spent for shoes? I hope she will be asked why she needed all of those shoes.

The whole town is now working together, but after two years, there was not much to show for it. Only a lot of hard work. Poor Mother had three more babies; Ili in 1948, with Magdi then Viki in 1950. Now we had one

25

more set of twins in the family. Poor Mother hardly survived that. Now we had nine girls and one boy.

In the commune, Father told the commune leader, the head Communist in Szarazd, that he was not fairly dividing the goods. The rest of the men agreed with Father. They said, "Alex beat him up." Well, Father slapped him. Mr. Marcis reported Father, and they locked him up. That was a big tragedy, because Mother needed him at home. She was scared to death as to what she was going to do with all of those children alone.

The neighbor lady, Mrs. Kupas, said she knew the judge. She took Mother to him and asked him to have Father sent home because he was needed at home, and Mr. Marcis was very unfair. The judge said he understood, but you could not hit the Communist Party head man. But he agreed to try to help. After six months, Father came home from the jail in very bad condition, mentally and physically. He went to work for the railroad.

John was fifteen years old. During the night, he plowed the ground with a tractor. Mother worried that he would fall asleep and the tractor would turn over on him. The reason it was done at night time was because the tractor was needed during the day some place else. It looked like the more work we did, the less we had.

They had taken all of the German people out of the country and, in their place, they relocated Hungarians from Yugoslavia. Now there were a lot of young people in the town. They organized dancing on Saturdays. Anna and I were too young to go dancing. Mother didn't let us go.

In 1949, when it was time to harvest the wheat, the men cut the wheat by hand using a scythe. Then the wheat was tied with a rope into bundles. These bundles were placed together with the wheat standing up into shocks throughout the field. When the threshing machine came, we got the wheat out of the fields using horse-drawn wagons. We only had one monstrous threshing machine in the town. It used a steam tractor to drive a giant belt to turn the thresher machinery. It was set up in about five different places around town.

Mother said it would be good if Anna and I could get a job on the threshing machine. We would be able to get enough flour so we could have bread for the whole winter. Mother said she would talk to Mr. Kovacs, but Mr. Kovacs did not want to hire Anne and me as he said we were way too young. We were only thirteen years old. "That is very hard work," he said.

Mother said, "But we are used to hard work." Mother asked Mr. Kovacs if he would try us out. We needed the flour for the winter bread, very much. Mr. Kovacs very reluctantly said okay.

For the next six weeks, Ann and I worked on the threshing machine. From six in the morning till six at night, we worked. Ann's job was up on top of the threshing machine where she would cut the ropes off of the bundles and throw them down into a hole in the machine. Ann almost fell into the threshing machine one morning. We were very happy when that job was done.

Now we had wheat to take to the next town to the flour mill. For two months, nobody had any flour to bake bread; Mother substituted the flour with corn meal. Since I was allergic to it, and there had been no bread for two months, I got skinny. Mother told me, "Don't worry; very soon we will have wheat to take to the flour mill, then I am going to bake delicious bread. But, until then, please try to eat the corn meal." I couldn't. It stuck up on the roof of my mouth. It was so wonderful when Mother was able to bake bread for us again.

September came. The school is from eight in the morning till one in the afternoon, and we are going to our favorite teacher—Mr. Bush. We loved his teaching.

From the commune farming, almost everybody finally got out of it. We got back some of our land. One night, Father said, "Next year, we are going to farm tobacco." He thought it was going to pay well. The new regime forced the people to farm cotton. But, the climate wasn't suitable for cotton farming. All of the work was wasted. So, therefore, we farmed tobacco for the next few years.

In springtime, we had to plant the tobacco plants which Mother had grown outside in beds, covered with plastic. We then had to take the small tobacco plants out to the field to plant and water them, one by one. By September, they were ready to harvest. The harvesting was done by picking the bottom leaves, because they were the bigger ones. The three of us—John, Anne, and I—five in the morning, had to go out to the tobacco field and harvest a wagon full of tobacco leaves. In the morning, everything was covered with dew. We got all wet and it was most uncomfortable. We had to be home and have enough time to put the harvested tobacco in the barn, have breakfast, and be at school by eight.

Chapter 9

1951: Sztalinvaros is Built

John went to Sztalinvaros to work. Sztalinvaros was a new city where they were building a new city close to the Danube. They were building a new steel mill there. They were building temporary housing for the workers. In the meantime, they were building the city. From all over the country, people went to work there. The young people from Szarazd were of the age to get their draft card to join the military. My boyfriend, Geza, was going, too. We made a big party for the boys. They said goodbye to their girlfriends and went to the military. The town was practically emptied out. Not many young people were left in it. Mother was thinking where I could go to work and earn some money. I was practically sixteen years old.

In 1952, Joe came home from the army to visit his parents. He came to visit us, too. He told us he was in Budapest. He liked it very much. He was able to see his sister since she lived in Budapest, too. My mother said, "Joe, would you take Elizabeth with you to Budapest and you and your sister find a job for her?" Joe didn't think that was a good idea but Mother kept insisting. Joe reluctantly agreed. The next day, Joe and I were on our way to Budapest.

Chapter 10

1952: The Budapest Canning Factory

Joe said, "We are going to Mrs. Major's house." Joe used to live with her as a tenant. Joe introduced me to Mrs. Major, and he told her I was there to find a job. He said he would appreciate it if she could help and told her that I would be living with her.

Mrs. Major said, "Maybe a can factory."

Joe said that sounded good and asked if she would take me to the employment office. She said she would. Then Joe said goodbye and I never saw him again. Before that, he said, "Here is my sister's address. In case you need help, she will help you."

I unpacked the food Mother packed me—hard boiled eggs, biscuits, bread, and a piece of cheese. Mrs. Major and I ate most of that for supper. She said I should give her money for the rent. When I gave her the money she asked for, I hardly had any money left. I thought maybe it would be enough for bread. Mrs. Major said, "We should go to bed." We will be leaving early to find you a job. The street car leaves at seven in the morning."

I went to bed gladly. That house was way too quiet and empty for me, compared with our house. There were ten of us kids in our house and it was very lively all the time. That was what I was used to.

That Monday night was very long. I felt extremely alone. I wondered, *How did I get here? How is my life going to be after this?* Who would be able to tolerate that terrible loneliness? What was my mother thinking, to send me into that strange place? I didn't understand the whole thing.

Mrs. Major said, "We are leaving in ten minutes—the street car will be here." I never saw a street car before. When I saw it, I thought, *That is a good way to get around.*

The street car stopped in front of a pretty big building. Mrs. Major said, "There is the place where they are hiring for the can factory." I didn't have much knowledge as to what they did in a can factory, but we were already here.

We went in. They took an x-ray. The doctor listened to my back and chest. After my examination, he said, "Young lady, everything is all right, except your heart is bigger than it should be and make sure you don't work hard."

And I answered him "Yes, Doctor."

In the meantime, Mrs. Major was waiting for me. She said we had to come back tomorrow for the rest of the examination.

We went home with the street car. Mrs. Major said, after we got home, "I saw in your package a little cheese. I could cook some noodles and we could have noodles and cheese for supper." I right away gave her the piece of cheese. She cooked the noodles and grated the cheese on it. We had supper. Mrs. Major said, "We need to go to bed. We will be leaving early in the morning."

I was hoping that night would be better, but it was not so. My loneliness was bigger than the last night. It seemed to me I had left home a year ago. I thought, *Does my mother have any idea what she has done? Send me to the strange world? I can't live this way. And what do I know about the can factory?*

I must have fallen asleep. I heard Mrs. Major yelling. "Get up, get up! The street car is coming!" I jumped out of the bed, and put my clothes on. At 8:00 AM, the street car stopped in front of the big building. Mrs. Major said, "Let's stand in the line. Hurry!"

Then she took me in a room. They gave me a little glass to get a urine sample. They gave me another dish for the other sample. I said, "Wow! That is not that easy, since I am constipated most of the time." The next three hours, I tried and tried. Mrs. Major was waiting. Then I turned the samples in and I was looking for Mrs. Major. I was anxious to tell her that, finally, I had had success and all of the examination was done.

The canning factory said they would let me know when I will be able to go to work. But I couldn't find Mrs. Major anywhere. After two hours waiting, I figured she got tired and went home. I remembered which street car we went home on yesterday. I thought, *I had better go home. She is probably waiting for me there.* When I got to the house, she was nowhere to be found. I figured I shouldn't go anywhere. We would probably miss each other. It was better for me to stay here and wait for her. One hour later, Mrs. Major came home. As soon as she saw me, she started really yelling. I could tell she was extremely angry and upset. She started yelling at me. She was not going to help me. I was a bad girl. I was running around. I tried to tell her I waited for her for two hours right where she was supposed to be. But she was way too angry to hear me.

That night, I still had one biscuit Mother packed me. I ate it, since I had had nothing to eat all day. Finally, Mrs. Major calmed down. She told me she had gone shopping and it took much longer than she thought it would. She heard I passed all of the examinations and that the factory would let us know when they want me to come to work.

On the third night, I thought about how wonderful it would be to be at home. I wondered what Mother and everybody was doing. I wondered if Mother knew how orphaned I felt here. Mrs. Major even yelled at me here. Mother never yelled at me. I was her right hand. I wasn't a bad girl, like Mrs. Major was saying. I thought I had better go to bed. That night was worse than the other two. My homesickness was unbearable. *What would happen to me here?* Around midnight, I decided I was not going to stay here. I remembered Joe had given me his sister's address and told me that if I needed help to go to her. I planned out that in the morning I would go and look her up. Then I settled down. I was seeing solutions out of that horrible nightmare.

In the morning, I told Mrs. Major that I was going to go see Joseph's sister. She said to me, "All right." She told me which street car would take me there.

I found the place without any problem. When I rang the doorbell, a very nice woman opened the door. I told her that Joseph said his sister lived here and if I needed help to come to her. She asked me into the apartment. She asked me if I were thirsty. I was thirsty *and* hungry, but I told her, "Yes, I am thirsty."

She gave me a glass of soda and a pastry. Then she asked me, "How do you like Budapest?" I asked her when Joseph's sister would come home. Mrs. Marcis Irenke said she really didn't know, since she spent a lot of time at her boyfriend's place. Again, Irenke asked, "Do you like Budapest?"

I told her, "Not very much." Then I told her I had decided I was not going to stay in Budapest.

Then Irenke said, "Where are you going?"

I told her, "I am going home. But, I am not sure if I have enough money for a train ticket. I would be ever grateful if you would lend me the additional money I need for the ticket to take me to Sztalinvaros, since my brother lives there. As soon as I get home, I will send you the money back."

Irenke knew I was very homesick. Irenke was from Yugoslavia, and married to a Hungarian man. She understood how homesick I was. She also knew Budapest was too much for me at once. She said, "We will go to the train station and find out how much the train ticket costs to go to Sztalinvaros. We also need to find out when the train is leaving."

She would give me the rest of the money so I could go home. I don't have to tell you how happy I was! Irenke told me to go back to Mrs. Major and tell her I was not staying in Budapest, as I had decided to go back home. She said that I should bring my stuff back with me.

Mrs. Major said, "I understand."

Irenke's apartment was closer to the train station. The train would leave the next morning at eight. No one, but no one, was happier than me in the whole wide world.

I also told Mrs. Major that, if everything went well, I would be home by the next night. I got my little stuff, said goodbye to Mrs. Major, and I was on my way to Irenke's house. Her husband was already home. Dinner was offered to me. By that time, I was very hungry. The hot food tasted very good. Irenke showed me the bed I was to sleep in. I went to bed very relaxed. Three nights with very little sleep really wore me out. I fell asleep right away.

In the morning, Irenke fixed us breakfast—coffee and pastry. And we left for the train station. The train came shortly, and I said goodbye to Irenke. I never saw Irenke ever again, and I think of her with a lot of love, that wonderful woman. I wished her a life lived happily.

Chapter 11

1952: I Moved to Sztalinvaros

Mid-morning the next day, I arrived in Sztalinvaros. I knew where my brother lived. He was in a military-like service that wore black uniforms and guarded the secrets of the steel mill still under construction. I got to the barracks where they were living. I said to the guard, "I am looking for Kertesz John."

He went into the building and I heard them yelling, "Kertesz, a good-looking chick is looking for you."

My brother anxiously came. He said, "You crazy? She is not a chick; she is my sister." Then he turned to me and, surprisingly, asked me, "What are you doing here?"

I started to tell him that Mother had sent me to Budapest with Joseph and I was going to work there. My brother interrupted, "But, what are you doing here?"

I said, "I didn't like it in Budapest. I decided to go back home."

He said, "Yeah, yeah, but what are you doing here?"

I said, "But you know I have no money for a train ticket. You need to give me some money so I can go home."

He said, "You wait a minute here; I will be right back." A few minutes later, he said, "Now, we can go."

I was very surprised and I said, "Go where? Where are we going?"

"I am going to show you that new city. That street is called the crooked street; see how crooked it is? You see that third building? That is where the girls live. In this city, the young people are working here. When it is completed, this city will have twenty thousand people living here."

I thought, *Wow*! That is a large city, especially when compared with Szarazd, which has only a hundred and ten houses.

Shortly after that, we were in the Steel Mill Street. He turned to me and said, "The reason why they named that Steel Mill Street is because, way over there on the end, they are building a steel mill factory. There they are going to manufacture steel." Going further, he said, "Look at that! Here, they are building the movie theater called Dozsa. A year from now, it will be completed. And over here, there will be a big hotel, which will be called The Golden Star."

We never had any need for hotels. It didn't mean very much to me. I told John, "Now I have seen a whole lot of things. Please give me the money, because all of the trains are going to leave and I want to get home before evening."

He said, "There is plenty of time and I want to show you something else, too." We stopped in front of a building. He said, "Wait here; I will be right back." Almost fifteen minutes later, he came back with a young woman, and they told me I had a job to go to work.

I said, "I am not looking for a job; I want to go home!"

My brother said, "It would be better; you have to stay here. Do you see the crooked street, the third building? That is where the girls live, and you will live there, too. Come on, we will show you."

They took me into the building. It was a big room. There were beds everywhere, at least six of them, with very thin mattresses and blankets like military blankets. My brother said, "That third bed will be yours. Tomorrow, you are going to work."

I was surprised, and asked, "Where? And doing what?"

"Here, not too far," my brother said.

"But what am I going to work at?"

Finally, he reluctantly said, "Peeling potatoes."

I just stood there. I couldn't believe what was happening to me. I turned to my brother and I said clearly to him, "But, I want to go home."

My brother said, "Now, I will take you to show you where you will be working." It wasn't far. It was a very large, flat building. We went in. He introduced me to a woman. It looked like they knew each other. He said, "Elizabeth, she is my sister, she will be coming here to work."

The woman asked, "Which section?" There was a big kitchen. They cooked for several thousand people.

My brother said to her, "She will be cleaning potatoes."

She said, "I will show you." She took us in a fairly large room. There were about eight or ten women there. I was introduced to them as the new girl. Everything happened so quickly.

That is how I started my life in Sztalinvaros. It seemed like I was in a dream. Of course, I couldn't go home without money. Many years later, I found out John didn't even have a penny. That was the reason I became a citizen of Sztalinvaros.

The next day, I went to work. The girls were very nice and kind to me. We were given a ticket and we got lunch for it. They deducted it from our pay. It was very good, hot, food. A machine peeled the potatoes, but didn't take out the eyes. The girls showed me how to finish cleaning the potatoes, and how to cut them into about four pieces, depending on the size of the potatoes. We got paid according to how many baskets of potatoes we did. At lunch time, we sat at long tables and we had lunch together. We talked and we laughed and we joked like young people do. I had to go to work at six in the morning.

The girls in the room were also very helpful and nice to me. The next morning, I was very glad to go to work. I thought, *This is not so bad; much better than in Budapest.* But I was also thinking, *I can't wait to go home. It is already a whole week and I haven't seen Mother and my sisters. I miss them so very, very, much.*

On Saturday, my brother asked me how I was. I said to him, "I am fine! But I would have been better if I had been able to go home."

He said to me, "Don't worry; next week we are going home."

I asked John, "Are you sure? Are you sure?" I was so happy, like a child who was promised candy.

At the end of the week, the girls and I went for a walk on the Steel Mill Street. Those who didn't go home were on the sidewalk on the Steel Mill Street, as it was the main street of Sztalinvaros. That is where the people saw each other and got to know each other.

On Monday, I went to work. I said, "Today is my birthday; now I am practically a grownup. I am sixteen years old!" I thought, *I don't know anything.* In Szarazd, we worked in the field from the time we were eight years old. In school, we learned 2 x 2 = 4, and who discovered America, but not much else. Well, cleaning potatoes might not be so bad. I was in Sztalinvaros a whole week. I liked the co-workers, I liked my room mates, and John promised we were going home the next weekend. Oh, I couldn't wait. I was so homesick. I thought, *Two days, and we are leaving. I hardly can wait. Poor Mother, she is probably going to be at the gate. She is going to wait for us. I am sure she is missing me, too.* She always said that I was her right hand. She needed a lot of help with so many children, and I helped her gladly.

Finally, we were on our way home. Just like I thought, Mother was waiting for us at the gate. As soon as we went into the house, I started telling her how terrible it was for me in Budapest. I asked her why she sent me there. She held my shoulder and said, "My little girl, there is nothing here. I was hoping and thought maybe you would have a better future there. Since your father picked this little nothing town, none of you has a future here."

How right she was. Mother spent the next sixteen years trying to get all of her daughters out of that town.

Mother's cooking was the best in the whole wide world! She made chicken paprikas with happy chickens. We had a big kitchen table. All twelve of us sat around it. My little sisters kept looking at me. They said, "Elizabeth, you look the same as you looked before you left." It must have seemed to them, too, that I had left a long time ago.

I told Mother how nice my room mates were and that the co-workers were very nice, too. Mother reassured me it would be all right, "You will see," she said. "You will get used to it. Then you can come home and visit."

I said, "Yes, Mother. I will come home every weekend."

I shouldn't forget my boyfriend, Geza. He was coming home the next weekend from the military.

On Sunday morning, I woke well-rested. I heard Mother calling the chickens. As we stepped out from our kitchen door, the flower garden and the well were right straight out from our kitchen door. The garden was covered with flowers, and the big yard was swept up nicely; Father demanded that. Mother was right, it was a very small town, but to me it was the most beautiful place in the whole wide world.

Mother interrupted my thoughts. She said, "Which one should we cook today? I am going to make rice with the chicken and vegetable soup."

I pointed at one chicken, "That one over there."

"Very well, come and help me. We have to hurry. The train is coming in the afternoon and you will have to leave."

Since I knew I would be able to come home every weekend, life didn't seem so tragic anymore. Mother came with us to the train station. The train shortly came. We said goodbye and we were on our way to Sztalinvaros.

After three months of cleaning potatoes, I was told I was going to have a new job. I would be a new server, starting the beginning of the next week. Well, that was good, and it wasn't. It was good because I was going to be paid a regular payment. The potato cleaning was paid by how much I produced. I wasn't good at it, so I made very little money, since my hands weren't used to working fast. My hands were used to heavy work, plus, my potatoes had to be very clean. The serving job was out of the city, and I had to move over there. That was where the construction workers making the steel mill were living in barracks. They ate in mess halls with long tables set up where they were served breakfast, lunch, and supper. So I made a move.

Five of us were living in a room. New place, new room mates, not bad. Of course, by then, I was tolerating change much better. I liked my new room mates.

Monday morning, they said, "The workers will be here in fifteen minutes and we should hurry up to set the tables." The girl said, "They are coming. The men are here."

Wow! I never saw so many handsome, good looking, young men in my whole life! By the next day, four young men asked me to go dancing with them! I chose Miska. The friendship didn't last long. He always wanted to make love to me. Now Feri, he was the handsomest young man I ever laid eyes on. He wanted to make love with me, too. There was Antal, handsome, intelligent, and a crane operator. The new regime didn't allow him to continue his doctor's education because his father was considered by the new Communist regime to be a bourgeoisie. So, therefore, Antal was operating the crane.

I started dating Antal. He walked me home one late afternoon. He was telling me my eyebrows were a little too thick, and we should make them thinner. He could do it. I said okay. He held my head, my face. He even kissed me. And I suddenly realized we were in bed. Of course, right away, I thought, *Oh my gosh, I hope there is not going to be trouble out of that. What would Mother think?* I never got too close to Antal after that. I resented him.

I met Jeno. I decided I was going to keep him. He was the most gorgeous man anybody laid eyes on. Not many men were as handsome as he. We started dating. After two months, I gave Jeno up. He was the most boring person on earth.

I was going home every weekend. I took all my money home and gave it to Mother.

I had lived in Sztalinvaros a year, when, at work, I met Andras. We sat together at lunch. I thought, *What a nice young man.* One day I was going on a date and ran into Andras, and he asked me where I was going. I told him, "I am going on a date."

He said "On a date?" He was very surprised. He told me that I was his girl friend.

I said, "I am very sorry, but I thought we were only friends."

He started crying. He said to me, "You just wait. You will be crying where no one can see you," and he ran away. I thought that was very strange.

The movie theater got built. The Gold Star Hotel was also built. They were two beautiful buildings. The Gold Star Hotel had two sides. I was asked to come and work there. I was no longer going home every weekend. I realized my clothes and shoes were very worn. I needed the money to buy new ones. Mother sent Anna to Sztalinvaros. My brother got her a job working in a coffee shop. Now, there were three of us in Sztalinvaros. The city was growing, too. All around from the surrounding villages and towns, people came to work here. Grandmas watched the children at home. There was a lot of opportunity to meet new people, and they did. The result of that was a lot of divorces.

The Steel Mill Street sidewalk was about twenty feet wide. After work, citizens of the city would stroll, getting to know each other. The other reason for strolling was that, in the rooming house, there was nothing to do. The room was filled up with iron beds. A little wooden radio hanging on the wall played, most all the time, music about how the famous, glorious, victorious, Russian Red, brave, soldiers liberated us.

If a new song came out and the Communist Party, after censoring it, gave their permission, it was played on the radio. I remember one new song came out. The title was "Every Woman's Life There Comes a Time She Would Love To Do What is Not Allowed." Everybody loved that new song, I think, because there was a lot of truth in it. Television was non-existent in Sztalinvaros, at that time. So, as you can see, this is why everybody went out strolling on that wide sidewalk.

The iron beds and the little wooden box called a radio did not keep the people in such a room. It seems to me the city planners knew there would be a great need for that very wide sidewalk.

In 1954, Anne met John. Although John was a good-looking man, he was also a very arrogant person. In spite of all, Anne was very much in love with him. By now, we seldom went home, because money was very scarce. We could hardly clothe ourselves, in spite of going hungry.

At home, Mother sent Juliska to an accountant's school. She would be the first one to be educated.

I met my life's biggest love. He was a young officer. We fell in love with each other right away. His name was Joseph. He told me, "From now on we are not to go out with anyone else." I agreed right away. He was perfect: his height, his skin, his blond hair, the way he smiled, the way he looked at me, the way he held me. Is that what love is? Then, I was very much in love. Not too long after that, I found out my very handsome boyfriend was in love with other girls, too! We had a lot of arguments about it. I had to realize he was not for me. He was not husband material.

Chapter 12

1955: A Steel Mill is Completed

In 1955, the steel mill was finished. The steel mill construction men left the city and they were replaced with about five thousand steel mill workers, who were going to operate the steel mill. The city lost some citizens and gained some. In the meantime, the city was building apartments. There were not enough for everybody. The city provided apartments first to married people with children. Unmarried people still had to live in the rooming houses. We also had nice clothing stores in the city. We had clubs to go dancing. We were going dancing.

My brother rented a room from Mr. Toth. Then he had to go to the army. He turned the rented room over to Anne and me. That way we didn't have to live in boarding houses. We were very happy for the room, even if it wasn't heated. It was very cold in the room. We couldn't even cook anything. That was okay, as there was nothing to cook, anyway. We went hungry all the time.

Our pay check was enough for a week and a half, instead of four weeks. We couldn't even go home anymore, just on the big holidays of Christmas and Easter. At home, life wasn't any better. Father was working very hard at the railroad. Mother was working in the fields growing vegetables and potatoes, etc. Szarazd had a little store.

Mother wrote that she could not purchase any lard to cook with. There was none at the store. Since Father was working in Sztalinvaros, too, he said to me, "I purchased about sixteen pounds of lard and I want you to help me by taking it out to the railroad station so I can take it home."

We had to cross a field like a football field to get to the railroad station. As we went, each of us was holding a side with a handle. Father said, "We have a problem."

I said, "What kind of problem?"

"Look, the police man is running after us."

I looked back. Yes, there was a police man running after us. The thing was, nobody was allowed to take lard and meat out of the city because it was needed for the city workers. There wasn't enough. When the police man was close enough to see me, he stopped and turned around. Father said, "Look, he stopped and he is turning away." He said, "I wonder why he is doing that."

I said to Father, "Because he wants a date with me."

Father said we were very lucky, as, if they had caught us, we would have been locked up.

We didn't have any money for the train. We wanted to go home very badly. I said to Anne, "Let us try it. Maybe the conductor will not ask for a ticket from us." She agreed and we boarded the train.

We talked it over. When the conductor came, he usually said, "Tickets please, where haven't I checked the tickets?" We acted like he already checked our ticket. We didn't pay any attention to him. We talked like we were very busy. When he left our cabin, we looked at each other and said, "It worked!"

At home, of course, we didn't tell Mother how we got home. And we still had to get back. Mother was very happy we had come. My little sisters looked at us, waiting to find out what we had brought them. When they saw we had not brought them anything, their little faces were so sad.

Mother was forty-three years old. She looked like sixty-three. She worked so much. All that work was destroying her. My little sisters looked neglected. Everybody was poor and hungry, although the war had been over for ten years.

When they brought some meat into the cities, you had to stand in long lines. By half of the line, the store usually ran out of meat, even when the people were purchasing only one pound. Everything was very expensive. We were not allowed to complain. Those who dared to were the enemy of Communism. They took them away and they never came back home. Therefore, the people silently bore it.

We had no heating, no hot water, nothing to heat with. Although we had a heating stove in our room, but there was nothing to heat with. The winter was very cold. Anne and I cuddled in the cold bed. Her knees hurt terribly. The only way she could sleep was to put her knee into my back. I felt sorry for her, very much.

In September 1955, I was working in the afternoon. Soon, I took my place behind the counter. A tall, blond, young man came in to the restaurant. While he was eating his lunch, he constantly watched me. After lunch, he came to me. He introduced himself to me and he asked me to go dance with him that night. I told him, "I can't, I am working."

He asked, "How long?"

I said, "Until ten."

He said, "That is all right. I will wait for you in the Golden Star."

I told him, "Don't wait, because I am not coming."

But he stood there and begged me. And he said he was not leaving until I said yes.

Since I was working, it was very unpleasant to deal with him. Just to get rid of him, I said, "All right! After work, I will see you."

He said goodbye and left.

Of course, I had no intention to see him. I was still very much in love with Joseph. I already decided that he was not for me, but love is love. At ten in the evening, we closed up the restaurant and I was on my way home. I almost made it home.

I noticed someone running after me. He said, "Why didn't you meet me? You promised!"

I said to him, "I don't know you. You were bothering me in my work place."

He asked for my forgiveness and he said, "Let's start all over." My name is Laszlo Dobosi. I am a house painter and a furniture finisher. You would make me very happy if you would come back to the Gold Star with me to dance. The evening is still young. It is a beautiful first of September and I love to dance."

Since I loved to dance, too, I let him talk me into it, and we went dancing. It was live music everywhere, and a beautiful dance floor. Laszlo and I danced. He said, "Elizabeth, would you allow me to introduce you to my friends?"

I said, "That is fine."

He took me to the table. About eight guys were sitting there. He said to them, "Look, guys, I found a girl who will be my wife."

Of course, they looked surprised. Me, too. One of them said, "Are you crazy?"

He answered, "Not at all." I couldn't figure what to make out of the whole thing.

While we were dancing, he said, "Would you be my wife?"

I looked at him and wondered, *Who is this young man?* He danced very well. At the end of the dance, he walked me home. I thought, *Now, I am really going to find out who that man is.* He behaved like a gentleman. He told me where he was from, and how many sisters he had. Then, he asked me if he could come see me tomorrow after work.

It was two in the morning. I told him yes. He was very entertaining.

On our third date, he asked me, "Would it be okay if we get married on the 10th?" So far, all I knew was that I was having a wonderful time with him. Every day, right after work, he came to see me. Laszlo said, "You know, we have to register in the city hall." He said, "I will take care of everything. Tell me where you were born." I told him the name of the town where I was born. By the time he got to the city hall, he forgot it. The third time, Anne and I wrote it down for him.

The town I was born in was Gyergyoalfalu. He registered us in the city hall.

Chapter 13

September 10, 1955: I Married Laszlo Dobosi

On September 10, 1955, Laszlo Dobosi and I got married. It was ten days after our first date. Anne moved in with her boy friend, John. Laszlo and I lived in that rented room. I was very happy with Laszlo. My husband was decent, and a hard working man. I saw that. That is why I came to be his wife.

When we had been married for two weeks, a terrible thing happened. I lost my job. The reason it was so terrible is because there were no job opportunities in the city. Laszlo told me, "Don't worry, we should be all right from my pay check."

In October, Anne and John got married. John got transferred to a different city. John had a big motor bike. They came to say goodbye. Anne was sitting behind John. I remember how sad I was as I watched them disappear. I felt so very bad that they had left. We are twins. I felt she was going to have it bad where they were going, without a job for her and I was right. She went hungry a lot and I did also, in Sztalinvaros. Laszlo's paycheck wasn't enough for both of us to eat properly.

In December, Laszlo took me home to Baja to introduce me to his mother and five sisters. My mother-in-law said, "Stay next to each other." We did. She said, "Very good." She seemed satisfied. Only Laszlo's little niece, Shari, was very unhappy. From then on, she would have to share her beloved uncle with another woman. I took Laszlo home, too, and introduced him to my parents. They hoped he would be a good husband, since we had dated such a short time.

In February 1956, Anne and John came back from Keszthelyrol to Sztalinvaros. They rented a room from a girl she used to work with. I was very happy to see my twin sister again. There was one more news item; Anne was pregnant. That was not happy news. They were terribly poor.

Anne had a navy blue wool dress with pleats. It had a lot of material in it. We took it to the dress maker and she made Anne a pregnant dress out of it. That was what she wore the whole time she was pregnant.

One beautiful spring day, flowers were blooming everywhere. We were enjoying the warmth after the long winter. We were in love with our husbands. They were in love with us. Life was pretty, even though we were hungry most of the time. *Oh, it would be so nice to find some kind of work,* we thought.

I heard they were hiring at the cleaners. I ran over there right away and they hired the two of us. We would start the next day. We were both very happy. The woman told me she had been looking for a job for a year and a half, and they had two little children at home. I felt very sorry for her and for the poor, hungry, little children.

I had been working two months in the cleaner. The money was not much, but more than nothing. We were able to buy Laszlo two pairs of underwear. Our whole wardrobe was very poor.

On a Monday, I was at my job. The boss said he was extremely sorry, but he had to let the two of us go, since there is not enough work. He was very sorry. One thing was sure; the older workers weren't looking as kindly. Everybody was worried about their job.

In September 1956, Laszlo brought a very small pay check home. In spite of it all, he worked very hard. He said he felt very inadequate. He said, "I can't even support one wife." I reassured him that it was not his fault and he should not worry. I told Laszlo that I had two coats and I was going to sell one of them. Then he almost started crying. He said, "Now eleven years have passed since the war is over and we are so poor we have to sell the wife's coat."

My poor Anna, she was going hungry, too. Mrs. Toth said they needed the room and we needed to find some place else to live. Laszlo's company gave us a small room on Kossuth Lajos Street, number 2, on the third floor. The room was just big enough to put two iron beds in it and a small table with two chairs. That was all that fit in there. Oh, we were so happy for it! At least we would be able to cook something on a hot plate. The Toth's didn't let us do that because the electricity was too expensive.

I was not well. I often had a terrible stomach ache. I was very skinny. The doctor thought I might have a gall stone. I didn't even know what a gall stone was. We were able to sell one of my coats. At least we had a little money.

On October 15, 1956, I received a letter from my mother. She said that since I was not working, she really needed some help. Would I come home and help her out? I talked it over with Laszlo, and decided I would go home to help Mother out. At the end of the week, he would come over and we would come back to Sztalinvaros together. I arrived at Mother's house. I remember we had to harvest the sugar beets. The weather was cold and rainy. I was very cold, but we had to hurry up, as the weather would just get colder.

Chapter 14

October 23, 1956: Revolution!

On October 23, 1956, Father came home. He asked, "Have you heard about the news?" We hadn't heard anything. Father said the revolution had started in Budapest.

I said, "Then, tomorrow morning, I need to go back home to Sztalinvaros to be with my husband." Right away, we turned the radio on. The radio said there was a lot of shooting going on in Budapest. The people were together in the squares and demanding the Russians leave Hungary and they had to set up a democratic government. In Sztalinvaros, they also had a revolution.

Dobosi Laszlo, my husband, was one of the leaders. Nine of them wrote down the eleven demands the people had. Number one: the Russians must immediately leave Hungary. The revolution had spread all over the country. The government sent the Hungarian soldiers home, among them was my brother, John. Therefore, they left only the Russian soldiers.

A lot of shooting was going on in every city. We listened to the radio. That is how we were getting the news. We didn't leave the radio for one second. We heard the leadership of the revolution was asking for America to help. The news was, "Hold out, Hungarians, we are coming!" America was going to help.

The next morning, I said goodbye to my parents. I was on the way to the train station. I wanted to be with my husband. At the train station, the station master told me that there were no trains going anywhere. That was terrible! I had to go. I would take a bus. He said, "They are not going either." Sweet Jesus, I was stuck here! I felt that my husband needed me.

I had to go back to Mother's house. She saw how terribly sad I was. She said, "What is wrong?"

I told her, "Mother, no transportation. Nothing is moving, not even the busses. My God! Anna is at the end of her pregnancy. I won't be able to help her."

The days passed. The radio said, "People, put down the weapons. The government will meet your demands." The Russians were going to leave Hungary. In the country, the people were jubilant. Finally, after all of these years, Hungary was going to be free! The thrill was too soon. Some of the Russians left the country, but new ones came in with lots of tanks. They shot up the cities and the people in them.

In the meantime, I was still stuck in Szarazd. Help was not coming from anywhere, not even from America. They did promise.

Then they started to arrest the people. The people didn't have tanks to fight back. We heard from the people the last, urgent pleas for help. The radio went silent. The revolution ended.

In November 10, 1956, all we Hungarians wanted was freedom: nothing else. A big pickup truck came to Szarazd. I found out he was going to Budapest. I asked the chauffer to take me to Sztalinvaros; that was where I lived. I was extremely worried about my husband. The chauffer reluctantly agreed to take me with him.

We arrived in the early morning. The city looked deserted. I only saw a couple of women, dressed in black. I hurried to our little apartment, hoping I would find my husband there. I couldn't find him. I told myself, *He is at Anna's place.* They lived in the Steel Mill Street. I thought, *Five minutes and I will be right there.* I went as fast as I could, so I would be there as soon as possible. Such loneliness came over me.

I arrived at Anna's place. I was so happy when I saw that my twin sister was all right and also the baby, Zsa Zsa. There was my brother and my brother-in-law, but my Laszlo was nowhere. They said he had been there a few days ago. They hadn't seen him since.

They started arresting everyone who was involved in the revolution. I decided to go and look around in the city; maybe I would find out something that way. I ran into people who knew Laszlo. I asked, "Have you seen Laszlo?"

They said, "Not for a while."

Another person said, "Have you looked in the morgue?"

"No, I know he is not there."

Another acquaintance asked, "Where have you been?" I explained I had got stuck at Mother's place. He said, "Then, you don't know anything. Your husband was a big revolutionary. They are looking for him very much. I think they are going to hang him. He even let the political prisoners out of the jail."

I ran into Laszlo's friend who also was from Baja. I asked him, "What is happening?" He said he was going home to Baja. The company had told everybody to go home and take a vacation. The government was worried the people were gathering to try to make plans. Therefore, they sent everyone on vacation. He said, "There is not much transportation. Would you come to Baja with me? Maybe Laszlo is at his mother's house."

I was thinking that was where he was! I agreed. "All right, I am coming with you."

We got on the first bus.. About twenty minutes later, soldiers stopped the bus. They came on and asked everyone for identification. I think they were looking for weapons. They were funny-looking Russians. We hadn't seen this type before. They were the Mongol type. A few minutes later, they allowed the bus to proceed.

Gyuri said, "The next stop, we are going to get off." That is what we did. He said, "Look over there. There is a cargo truck. I am going to ask him where he is going."

Gyuri motioned for me to come on, come on, He was going to Baja. I thought, *What luck.* The driver said the Russian soldiers stopped him frequently. Since the truck was empty, he didn't anticipate problems. We could stand at the side. They usually just lifted up the canvas and looked in. Maybe they wouldn't even see us. We were stopped four times.

Finally, we were in Baja. Gyuri said to me, "It is twelve-thirty, and I will walk you to your mother-in-law's house."

It was one o'clock in the morning. My mother-in-law opened the gate. As soon as she saw me, she started crying. I asked, "Mamma, what is wrong?"

She said "My little girl, come on in, come on in." I said goodbye to Gyuri. In the house, Laszlo's sister, Gita, was awake, too. They told me, "It is too bad you didn't come yesterday. You would have seen Laszlo then. He was here. Yesterday morning, he left. He tried to leave Hungary at the Yugoslav border." They said he left me a message; that he loved me very much and, as soon as he could, he would come and get me. Again, I felt very alone.

My dear mother-in-law made a bed for me and we cried together. She covered me up. She said "Rest, my daughter. You look very tired."

I promised her that I would sleep, but I couldn't fall asleep. I keep thinking, *How could my husband leave without me?* We were so happy together. I could not imagine our life without each other.

I woke when the light came in the window. My mother-in-law was up already. She asked me if I were hungry. I hadn't eaten for two days, and I told her, "Yes, I am hungry."

She said she was baking potatoes and she had good bacon, too. Gita was up, too. She asked me where I had been. I told her I was at Mother's house. There was no transportation, so I couldn't go back to Sztalinvaros. She asked if anything happened there, too. I told her no, it was way too small a town.

Mamma said, "The breakfast is ready. Come to the table." The three of us sat at the table, and the baked potatoes and the bacon and the coffee were very good. We were almost halfway finished with the breakfast, when a shadow covered up the kitchen door, which was half glass. We wondered who was coming so early. The door opened. All three of us had our eyes on the door.

And who stepped in? My husband! I felt like some amazing miracle had happened. He sat down and started telling us he almost made it, but the Yugoslavian soldiers caught him and chased him back into Hungary. I knew that when the revolution is failed, the revolutionary has no place in his own country.

Barely ten minutes passed after my husband came in the door when Gita, his sister, started to argue with him. I don't remember the subject, but her brother was very hurt. He told me not to eat, but I thought, *I am very hungry and I am going to eat.*

After breakfast, I told my husband, "Let's go out to the yard." I needed to talk to him. I said, "I see we are not welcome here. We are going to my parents place in Szarazd. Nobody will hurt you there. Then we are going to figure out what to do."

He said, "But, what are we going with? There is no transportation. Nothing is moving anywhere."

I said, "I know. I came from Sztalinvaros yesterday." I was thinking that Baja was a pretty big city and they would find my husband there. It was best for us to leave there, anyway. I told Laszlo we were going to walk.

He said, "It is very far."

I said, "We have time."

We went back into the house. He told his mother we had decided to go to Szarazd. A half hour later, we were on our way. My sister-in-law waved goodbye, but she didn't ask what we were going to travel with.

On November 15, it was very cold. My forehead was extremely cold. I didn't have a hat. We were walking toward the wind. If I had had a hat, I would have pulled it down on my forehead. A pickup truck came by, and he stopped and asked where we were going. We said we were going toward Dombovar.

The man said, "Get on the truck." He could take us about ten kilometers. It was so very nice to get on that pickup truck. We got rested a little bit and got warmed up, too. The man said, "I am going to turn here."

He let us off, and we thanked him for his kindness. We said goodbye to him. It seemed like he didn't want to know much about us. He wished us good luck and he disappeared fast. At six o'clock that night, the weather tuned colder. One thing was very good. We were not going towards the wind.

Laszlo was a very talkative person. You weren't bored with him. He always had stories to tell. He said, "I am just realizing we could tie my shawl on your forehead."

I said, "That is wonderful. What a good idea." I felt my poor forehead was freezing to death.

Laszlo said to me, "Csori (the nickname he gave me), I think we are half way to Szarazd."

I didn't say anything, but I thought, *Is that all?*

We were going ahead. The weather was colder by the minute. But, we were going and going. Laszlo said, "I think the next town is Dombovar."

I was very happy. I had been there. I remembered that is where Father sold one of the horses. The gray horse. Then, the red horse had cried all night. He missed his partner. Father said next day he must go back to Dombovar. He had to buy back the gray horse, but he couldn't find the man he sold the horse to.

Laszlo said, "We are almost to Regon." Wow, that was wonderful. That meant we were almost home. Four kilometers, and there was Szarazd. I said, "I have to pee."

He said, "We haven't eaten or had anything to drink all day. I don't know how you need to pee."

I said to Laszlo, "Do you hear that?"

He said, "What?"

"The dogs are barking. Those are the Szarazd dogs."

We had come to the beginning of the village. It was a little bit past midnight and the restaurant was open until one. We would be there soon, so it would be open when we arrived. "I would like to have a glass of soda," I told Laszlo.

Laszlo said he would have a glass of beer. We were very thirsty. Oh, it tasted so good! Then we left right away, because in ten more minutes we would be home. It was very dark. We walked in the middle of the road. The rain used to come down on that street very wildly, so they put stone on the road.

At last, there we were, at Mother's house. Poor things, they were going to be so surprised, when, at one in the morning, we knocked on the door.

Father said, "Who is it?"

I said, "It is us, Father, Elizabeth."

He answered me back, "I am opening the door, right away." Mother lit the lamp, but we were already in the house.

They asked, "Where are you coming from and with what?"

"From Baja, and we walked."

"Wow! In that cold? That is very far."

"Yes, it is. It is ninety-eight kilometers. But we came ten kilometers with a truck."

My parents asked me what had happened the two days since I had left. When I told them what happened, they said, "Then you haven't rested much.

Laszlo told them he had tried to leave Hungary at the Yugoslav border but he couldn't make it. My parents said, "You will be in a good place here."

They listened to the radio, too. They knew Laszlo was in a lot of danger. Szarazd was a very small village. "Nobody comes here," Mother said. "Now, let's go to bed. You two must be exhausted."

"Yes, and very hungry, too."

Mother said, "Dear Jesus, I am so amazed you two walked that much in this cold weather. I forgot you two must be hungry, too." She said, "You should have some goulash," and the table was set.

The food was very good. My mother's cooking was the best in the whole wide world. After we ate, we went to bed. It felt so good to stretch out. We fell asleep right away.

At ten in the morning, the house was very quiet. Mother said she was going to make eggs for breakfast. I asked where the little girls were. Mother said, "They are in school. Father is in the restaurant." That was where they found out the news and discussed it.

I said, "I am going outside to the bathroom." As I stepped on the ground, the bottoms of my feet were extremely painful. I was only able to walk on the side of my feet. It would take a couple of days to get well. Laszlo's feet hurt, too.

Father came home with the news. The whole country was surrounded with Russian soldiers.

I said, "I saw them in Sztalinvaros. They stopped the bus and asked for identification for everyone."

Father said, "We don't need to be worried; just rest."

Mother cooked lunch. The girls were home from school, too. Father said, "After lunch, we are going to work on our tobacco." The girls weren't happy about it. That was what they did every afternoon.

Julia couldn't go back to school. There was still no transportation. So, she was home, too. Maria was fourteen years old, Gizi was eleven, and Rozsa was ten. Ili was nine, and Victoria and Magdi (the twins) were six years old. Laszlo told them stories. They were amazed at how tall their brother-in-law was. They put their hands into his shoes, and only their shoulders showed! They found that very funny.

The first week of December 1956, transportation started to work again. We discussed that I would go back to Sztalinvaros to see what was happening. I arrived at Anna's place, and they were fine. They told me they had arrested the revolutionaries. They took them away. And they were looking for Laszlo. They asked if I had seen him. I thought I had better not say anything.

I walked on the street and ran across people we knew. They asked the same thing. "Do you know where Laszlo is?"

I said, "I don't know, I am looking for him."

Some of the people said, "Maybe they took him away to Budapest." They were taking those there who were the leaders in the revolution.

The more I went, the more I saw. I came to the conclusion we had to leave the country as soon as possible. But, we had no money. Then I had a thought. *I should go to Laszlo's company.* I thought it would be worth a try. I went to the office and I asked, "May I see Laszlo's boss?" The secretary said I should have a seat and she left.

About five minutes passed. Then she came back with a man. He asked me, "What can I do for you?"

I introduced myself. "I am Mrs. Dobosi. I can't find my husband anywhere. I don't have any money. I was wondering if the company owes him any money. I would be very grateful if you would check it out."

The man was very kind, and he said he would look into it. He told me to just sit there. A half hour later, he came back. He said I should follow him. He seated me and he handed over five thousand forint. He said that was all he was able to find. "And, in case you know where you husband is," he said quietly, "he has to leave from here." He asked me if I understood.

I told him, "Yes, I do." I said goodbye to him. Now I was very sure my husband had no place in his country. I went back to our little room. I gathered up what I could not take with me, and I took it to Anna's place. I told her I would leave that stuff there, and go to live with Mother for a while. I went back to our little room, and I put our clothes in a sheet, since we had no suitcase. I said goodbye to our little room. In spite of everything, Laszlo and I were very happy in there. I turned in the key to the building superintendent. If I hurried, I would be able to catch the afternoon train. And if everything went well, I would be at Mother's by supper time.

It had been a very tiring three days. Laszlo and Mother were very happy when I arrived. Of course, they were very anxious for me to tell them what was going on there in Sztalinvaros. I told them the news was not good. After supper, we would discuss it. My little sisters were sent to bed. The four of us sat at the kitchen table: Laszlo, Mother, and Father. Then I started to tell them Laszlo and I must leave the country, maybe towards Austria, since my uncle lived in Gyor, not too far from Austria. We thought maybe that was the way to go.

I said, "By the way, I brought some money." All three of them, at the same time, asked me where I had got the money. I said, "From Laszlo's company."

They asked me, "How much?"

"Five thousand forint."

Laszlo said, "That is two months pay! How did you do that?"

I felt my guardian angel was with me. This was miracle number one! They were absolutely amazed; it was indeed a miracle. I said we should leave the next day. Then it was decided. My poor mother started to cry. I said, "We must try."

Father said he would take the tobacco to the factory the next day. He was going to bring some money and cigarettes, because, at that time, we were smokers.

I told Father we must leave at the noon train. Then we decided to go to bed.

Chapter 15

December 5, 1956: Our Escape Attempts

The next morning, I kissed my little sisters before they went to school. Maybe for a while I would not see them. Father was leaving with the tobacco on the wagon, and he stopped in front of the kitchen door. I stepped on the wagon and said to him, "I must say goodbye."

Father said, "Don't leave. I will be right back. Wait for me."

I told him, "It is not possible. The time is too late. It is already December 5."

He said one more time, "I will hurry home." He pulled the reins on the horses and he left.

Mother said, "I am going to prepare some food for the train." We had one hour before the train arrived. My beloved mother walked out with us to the train station. She told us which train we changed over to in Budapest to go to Gyorszentivanon, where my uncle lived.

The train came shortly. We said goodbye to my beloved mother. Both of us were crying. We didn't know what the future held for us. And then the train was there.

We made ourselves comfortable in the cabin. Laszlo turned to me and said, "Elizabeth, who is this Uncle Steve we are going to?"

Of course, Laszlo didn't know them. He was Mother's younger brother. During the war, they lost each other. I remember when we lived in the number 9 house, we were outside in the yard and the postman came. He brought us a post card. Mother started reading it. She started screaming, "Jesus Maria! He is here, he is here. So close by." She was absolutely overwhelmed.

Father said, "Who is here?" He asked again, "Who is here?"

She said, "Steve, my little brother." We had no idea how close he was."
She said to Father, "Hitch up the horses! Let's go see him."

Father took the post card out of her hands. He said, "Victoria, we can't
go there with horses and wagon."

Mother said, "Of course we can. It is in the next town, five kilometers."

Father said, "Victoria, he is not in Gyonk."

"She said, "Where is he?"

Father said "Gyor."

Mother broke down. She said, "Oh. But right away we are going to
write."

My uncle said on the post card that, when we received it, we should
write to him right away, and he would come. The answer was written. One
of us had to run with it to the post office to mail it right away.

Then I told Laszlo, "You know, he was a police man in Gyor. He was
looking for us through the Red Cross. That is how he found us. Imagine
it, two weeks later he was at our house. They hadn't seen each other for
four years. Such happiness! My Uncle Steve, since he got married to Jolan, has lived with Jolan's parents. They are very nice people, and Kathy is
such a great story teller. Her husband is, too. You will see and you will like
them."

We were soon in Budapest. We had to ask the conductor how long we
had to wait for our connection. We could drink something in the train station. I was very thirsty. The conductor said, "Forty minutes."

That meant we would be there at eight o'clock. They would be so surprised, since they didn't know we were coming. Of course, we were living
in an unusual time. There were a lot of people in the train station. Oh, the
soda really tasted good! We ate some of mother's biscuits. A very good idea.
Ten minutes and the train would be there. We stood outside to make sure
we didn't miss the train and we could get a place to sit.

The train arrived, and we boarded it. The cabin was very pleasant, and
warm, too. My poor husband was very quiet. It hurt him terribly that we
couldn't free our beloved country. What would happen to Hungary and the

Hungarians? How many people would have to flee? How many would they put in jail? How many would be executed? Where would we wind up? It seemed like there was a lot of suffering ahead of us.

We arrived at Gyorszentivanon. "Come on, Laszlo. Let's not get there too late."

I knocked on the door. My uncle asked, "Who is it?"

"Elizabeth from Szarazd."

My uncle opened the door. He was so surprised. He said, "Come on in. Come on in."

I introduced them to my husband, the revolutionary. I added to it, "Now, we are refugees." The four of them just looked at us with much sorrow.

Jolan said, "I am sure you two are very hungry."

And we were. Right away, she set the dinner table. In the meantime, we told them we wanted to leave the country through Austria.

My uncle, Steve, said, "Many people left the country through Austria." He said, "But, it is going to be very difficult, since it is so late after the revolution. There are a lot of Russian soldiers guarding the border. You should have come much earlier."

Laszlo said, "Leaving my country is the last resort."

My uncle said, "I understand. You can't do anything else. You did all you could. Then, tomorrow we are going to try."

Jolan said we should all go to bed. "I am sure you will have a very hard day tomorrow." Jolan made our bed.

Uncle Steve said, "Seven o'clock in the morning, the train leaves for Gyor. That is how I go to work in the linen factory." Since the new Communist regime was established in Hungary, the higher ranking police were let go. They were not trusted by the new regime. We said goodnight to everyone.

In the morning, Jolan made a very nice breakfast of bacon and eggs. Uncle Steve said we should hurry up, as there was not much time before the train arrived. We said goodbye to dear Jolan and her parents.

Uncle Steve said, "Look, we are already here in Gyor. I will get off here. You two stay on that train. That will take you near the Austrian border. God be with you." And he jumped off of the train.

The train was going very fast. I was wondering where our destiny was taking us. I already missed Mother and the girls. Laszlo said, "Are you thirsty? Let's go buy some drinks in the dining car."

"Good idea, Yes, I am very thirsty." I couldn't believe my eyes who we ran into. There were Peter and Imre from Szarazd. And their cousin from Budapest was there, too. I asked, "What are you guys doing going this way?"

Peter said, "We are going to the neighbors. And you?"

I answered, "We are, too."

Peter said, "In that case, let's go together." Imre said they knew a man who was going to help. It looked like we had some sort of hope. We were very happy. It is a very bad feeling when you are going and you don't know how to get there.

Two hours later, the boys said, "We are getting off here." We got off the train, and Peter walked over to a man and they were very seriously discussing something. Peter turned to us, and said, "He is charging one thousand forint a head. Is that okay with us?" Right away, we gave him the money.

The man said, "We have to wait until it gets dark."

Laszlo said, "It will be a few hours."

The man answered, "It is winter. It gets dark early. You can hang out in the train station. But better spread out so you don't draw attention."

Finally, it was dark, and the man motioned for us to follow him. We were walking in a wheat field that had been harvested. We were walking and walking. Then we walked on the edge of the forest. It seemed like we had been walking hours and hours. We asked the man, "Is it still far to the border?"

He said, "About two more hours."

It was very dark. We heard some sounds. The man said, "Bad news, Russian soldiers are around here. That is where we wanted to go over the border. Last week I took people over here. We have to turn back."

We said, "Oh, no!"

He said he didn't know any other place to go over the Austrian border. "I am sorry, but there is no other way. We just have to go back."

By seven in the morning, we found ourselves where we had started out. The man said, "If you hurry, you will be able to catch the train. It is going to Gyor. You will be able to go back to Gyor."

We said, "We do not want to go to Gyor. That is not where we want to go."

The man said goodbye and he left.

Laszlo, the boys, and I talked it over. On the train, we could get closer to the Austrian border. Laszlo said, "We need a map." Peter pulled a map out of his pocket. They checked the map, and picked out the name of a town which was close to the Austrian border. Next, we had to find out which train we should get on.

Laszlo said he would find out from the station master. A couple of minutes later, he came back. He said the train would leave five in the afternoon and it would stop at that town. Then it was decided. We were going together.

Peter said, "How are we going to spend the whole day?"

Laszlo said we should go into the town and find a place to have lunch. Imre asked jokingly "Who is sleepy?"

Peter said, "Now what do you think? Who could be sleepy, since we haven't slept all night."

Imre said, "I am only joking."

I said, "We will sleep on the train." We decided to separate. At five, we would meet in the train station.

In the town, there was a restaurant and we had lunch. We sat there until the restaurant owner started to look at us. Why were we still there? Laszlo thought it would be best to leave and go back to the train station. The boys were already there. In an hour and a half, the train would arrive. We sat down. We were tired. Everybody was busy with their own thoughts.

Finally, the train pulled into the train station. There was a lot of room on the train and it was comfortable and warm. An hour later, Imre said, "We are getting off here."

It was unusually dark. You seldom see such a dark night. Not a star in the sky—not one. We were going on some farm land. Peter said, "Now we have been walking about three hours. I wonder where we are." Soon after that, we heard voices.

Imre said, "These are Russians. Let's turn back." That is what we did. We couldn't do anything else. We found ourselves back in the train station. It was almost morning, and we were really tired.

I said to Laszlo, "Let's go back to Gyorszentivanon."

Peter said, "What is there?"

I said, "My uncle lives there."

The boys decided they were going to give up, and looked at us. I said, "We can't give up." We said goodbye, and went our separate ways.

Jolan opened the door. She looked at us with great sorrow. She said, "You two look like you need a week's rest." She said Uncle Steve would be home in a half an hour and told us, "We will have supper and you two go to bed."

We agreed to rest, and tomorrow start again. My uncle, Steve, got home, and we told him the past two days were not successful.

He said, "I am so sorry. Tomorrow, you two should rest."

We were in bed, and Laszlo said, "We should go to Budapest. No one knows us there."

I said, "Now what do you think? How long will it take before they find you?"

Laszlo said, "I am so sorry for you."

I reassured him. "You remember our wedding vows? You promised we would be together forever, in good and bad."

My husband said, "Do you know what? I love you very much."

"Me, too. Good night. Laszlo, do you know what tomorrow is? It is December 10th."

He said, "Really?"

"Yes. We are running out of time. Now let's go to sleep."

Jolan prepared a very nice breakfast. My uncle was getting ready to go to work. He said, "I am hurrying to make sure I will catch the train."

"Uncle Steve, we are going to take the afternoon train."

He said, "Maybe we will see each other there. I will be looking for you." Then he left.

Jolanka said, "I am going to cook a nice lunch."

We were very grateful. Jolan's father went out to the wine cellar. He said he had run out of the wine. He asked Laszlo if he wanted to go with him. They left. I helped Jolan with the lunch. Jolan's mother was telling stories. She had a lot of good stories and she knew how to tell them. The time was passing. It is already two in the afternoon. "As soon as Laszlo and my father get home, we are going to have lunch," Jolan said.

Kathy said, "We were just talking about you."

Jolan set the table. She said we needed to hurry. In half an hour, the train would arrive.

The train came in time, and we arrived in Gyor. We checked out which train was going toward Austria.

My uncle said, "Hello. That is the train you are going with?"

We said "Yes." But we felt very unsure. Should we go or shouldn't we go?" We'd had some very bad experiences the past few days. We were looking at my uncle. We asked, "Should we go?" But he didn't say anything. We said goodbye and we boarded the train.

As we stood in front of the cabins, wondering which way we should go, my eyes caught three young couples sitting in the cabin. I looked at their faces. I turned my back so they couldn't hear what I was going to tell Laszlo. I said, "Look at those couples in there. They are planning to do what we want to do."

My husband said, "Craziness."

I suggested that we stay with them.

My husband said, "And how are we going to do that?"

"We are going to do what they do. Don't ask them any questions. Let's sit in the cabin with them." This finding of the Jewish couples was our second miracle.

An hour later, they were getting ready to get off of the train. We got off, too. Everybody went into the train station. They sat on the benches. We sat on them, too, but not too close. I told Laszlo, "I am going to take off my shoes. I think there is a rock in it, which is hurting my feet." In the meantime, I watched every move they made. Fifteen minutes pass. They stopped eating and they ran out of the train station. I hadn't laced my shoes back, yet. I told Laszlo, "Run after them. Don't lose them."

I tied my shoes very fast and I ran out, too. Laszlo was standing out there all by himself. I was very upset. I asked Laszlo where they are. He said he didn't know. I argued, "What do you mean, you don't know? You came right after them."

"I don't know, they disappeared."

I kept arguing. "How could they disappear so fast? They must be here. Let's find them."

As we went behind the train station, there they were! They were discussing money with a driver. We stepped right between them. My husband heard how much money the driver was asking. He said, "Elizabeth, come on, we don't have that kind of money."

I kicked my husband on his shin. That means shut-up. I turned to the driver. I said to him, "Look, that is all we have—one thousand forint."

He said, "Get up on the truck." It was an open, big truck. It did have some sides. Although it was already evening, he said, "Make sure you stoop down so nobody sees you. A half an hour and we will be there."

We had no idea where we were going. About thirty minutes later, the truck stopped in front of a fairly big farm house. A woman came out of the house with a lamp in her hands. She said, "Quickly, come on in, come on in." We went into the house. It was a big farm house. She said, "Sit at the table. I am going to serve you dinner. You all must be hungry."

I started to figure out what was happening. I called my husband aside. I told him he absolutely should not ask any questions of anybody, and not talk, because these three couples came to that place which was already set up for them.

I hoped the people in the house were not going to find out that Laszlo and I just hitched ourselves to the three couples. We sat back at the table. It was a very good dinner: hot chicken soup, breaded pork chops, and mashed potatoes. The woman said, "There is plenty. Go ahead and eat." During the dinner, she said her husband was not home, but her brother was going to be our guide to take us to Austria. She recommended right after dinner that we all should go to bed and try to rest. After midnight, about one o'clock, we would leave.

We got in bed. I asked my husband, "Have you figured it out—what is going on here?"

Strangely, he asked me, "How did you know? How did you know when we got on the train that they wanted to flee the country, too?"

I said to my husband, "It was on their faces. Now, I hope they are not going to discover we hitched ourselves to them."

That was planned out for them. They knew where they were going. I said to my husband, "I know you love to talk, but now don't ask anything, and we hope they are not going to ask us anything, either.

My husband said, "It is two o'clock. Go to sleep."

I did fall asleep. I was awakened by the house lady. Gently, she said, "Time to wake up. In a half an hour, we are leaving. The coffee is ready." I couldn't believe our luck.

We thanked the lady of the house for everything. We said goodbye. Her brother asked, "Is everybody ready? Then we should be on our way." We walked on the harvested corn field; the night wasn't too cold. There were even a few stars in the sky. We started out the trip very optimistically. The man said, "In the morning, you will be on the other side." We hoped that would be so.

About forty minutes into our walk, we heard sounds. A tent had been made from the corn shocks. That was where the sounds were coming from. The man said, "We have a problem." From the corn shocks, they were playing with a flashlight. We all recognized the language. It was Russian.

On our left, there was a forest. The man started to run like a rabbit, and we were right behind him. When we were far enough into the forest, he explained to us that, just two days ago, he had been bringing people that way without any problem. He said, "Not too far from here there is a huge barn where they kept the straw and hay. We should try to get in there.

We made it to the barn. Soon after that, we heard vehicle noises. Also, they were shooting up flares so much it made that huge barn completely lit. The sound of the language made us completely sure they were Russians. We were also sure they captured a lot of people who were planning to leave the country. For a couple of hours, we were hearing "Pasli! Pasli!" (That means "Get going, get going.") We asked the man, "What do they do with these people they capture?" He said they take them to Budapest and they have to appear in court.

Hours later, it got very quiet outside.

The man asked, "Should we try again?" We didn't say anything. The man said, "That is all right, it will be light soon, anyway." He suggested we should sneak back to the house before it got light.

Finally, we reached the house. In the house, the man of the house was already home. He was very surprised when he looked at us. He asked his brother-in-law what had happened. The brother-in-law started explaining that when we got over there, a tent was made from the corn shocks and Russian soldiers were in it.

The man of the house said, "And what the hell were you doing over there? Didn't I tell you which way to go?"

He said, "I was thinking that would be all right, too."

The man of the house said, "Get out of my face. Go home!" Then he turned to us with a kind voice and he said he was very sorry. He apologized. Then, he said. "You should not worry one bit." He guaranteed us that, the next morning, we would be in Austria. He also said, "I am asking all of you not to go out of the house. We should not be seen by anyone. My wife will provide the food, anything you need. Your job will be to rest." He was very reassuring. We felt better right away. He also said, "Spend most of the time sleeping. We will leave after midnight, about one o'clock."

I thought, *Today is already December the 11. I do hope they are not going to shut down the border before we get through.* I didn't share that thought with my husband. I knew he was very concerned.

The day passed. It was evening, and the lady of the house served us a very nice dinner. The man of the house said, "We should get in bed soon. We have a lot of walking to do ahead of us." Later, we woke up to the smell of the coffee. We anxiously dressed. I am sure all of us were thinking, *Will we make it this time?* I also thought, *Now or never.*

It was December 12. We were on our way. I noticed what a pleasant, quiet night it was; not too dark, stars in the sky. The man said, "One more hour and we will be there."

I looked at my watch. We had been walking three hours. I turned to Laszlo and said to him, "I think we will make it this time."

All he said was, "Good."

One hour later, the man said, "Here we are." We were standing in front of a small ditch. It looked like not long ago it had been an iron fence. The man said, "You step over and you are in Austria! It will be four kilometers to the first town."

We had such a relief. We couldn't believe it! We kissed the man, hugged him, and shook his hands—and we stepped over that small ditch.

Chapter 16

December 12, 1956: Freedom in Austria!

December 12, 1956, 05:12 AM. This was the third time my guardian angels were with us. With such relief, we started towards the nearest Austrian town. Such a burden was lifted from our shoulders! Now Laszlo was able to ask anything he wanted to.

Pretty soon, we got to the first Austrian village. There were lots of tents, and also a lot of refugees. We asked them, "How long have you been here?" Some people said a month and a half; others said two months. We asked them what they were waiting for. They didn't know. Right away, we decided that was not for us. The more we looked, the less we liked what was in there.

One of our traveling companions, Udith, came up to us. She was bragging to her husband, "Look what I got!"

He asked, "What?"

Udith said, "Ten schillings."

"Who gave it to you?"

"A young man."

The other girl's husband said, "Kathy, put your lipstick on and go show yourself, too, and you might receive some money."

An hour later, we decided we should go to Vienna. We started out on foot. About an hour later, a fairly big station wagon was approaching. We put our hands up, and the vehicle stopped. The man asked where we were going.

We told him, "To Vienna."

He said they could pick up two couples. It was decided that Udith and her husband, and Laszlo and I would get a ride. The other two couples said, "Not to worry, somebody will pick us up, too." We said goodbye.

There was a three-year-old little girl in the vehicle. There was no talking since we didn't know each other's language; instead, there was a lot of smiling. In the late afternoon, we got to Vienna. We thanked the couple for their kindness for the ride. We said goodbye to Udith and her husband.

They were lucky; they had an address to go to. Therefore, they knew where they were going. Laszlo and I stood on the street in Vienna. We looked at each other, wondering which way to go. As we looked around, I said to Laszlo, "Look! I see a policeman over there. Maybe he knows where the Hungarian refugees are." We walked up to him. He understood what we were asking. He told us which street car we should take to get to the old hospital. That was where the Hungarian refugees were.

We understood and we told him we didn't have any money for the street car. He took his wallet out of his pocket and he gave us money for the street car.

Forty minutes later, we found the huge building. We found a room with a lot of long tables and benches. We were hoping we were not too late for supper. We didn't find anyone who was able to give us information. Where could we find food?

One man said, "What? You are looking for supper? Supper was over a long time ago." Then we realized it was after nine in the evening. Laszlo suggested we pull the benches together and sleep on them. In the morning, we would go to the American Embassy.

At eight in the morning, we were in the American Embassy. Laszlo went to the office and I was waiting in the lobby. In a short while, he came out. He asked me, "Should we go to America?" I said, "I really don't care where we go, as long as it is not far away." I was thinking that, as soon as the political situation got straightened out, we would go home.

My husband said to me, "Then, we are going to America!" Then he went back into the office. A short while later, he came out again. He sat down next to me. He said, "Look, we got two vouchers. We need to go to the train station. We are going to receive two train tickets to Salzburg. There is a big camp for the refugees and they will take us from there to America. They gave us some money for the bus to the train station."

We arrived at the train station. Laszlo went to the ticket window. I just stood about four yards away. As I stood there waiting for Laszlo, a man came up to me and he put one hundred schillings in my hands. This was our third miracle.

I looked at the money. I wanted to say thank you in German, but I was so stunned, I couldn't think of the words to say, "Danke Schon." In school, we had learned German. I yelled at Laszlo, "How do you say 'thank you' in German?" By the time I came to my senses, the man had disappeared.

Laszlo said, "Look, we got the train tickets." I showed him the hundred schillings. Of course, he asked me, "Where is that from?"

I said to him, "A man gave that to me."

We looked around in the room and saw a breakfast counter. We decided to have breakfast: coffee and croissant. While we were having breakfast, I thought, *My guardian angel is with us again. And we will be very careful with the money.*

Laszlo said, "You see the basket at the end of the counter? I am going to buy you a banana since you have never eaten a banana before."

I said, "We are not going to buy a banana. We are going to save that money, since we don't know what is in the future."

But he kept asking me to let him buy me a banana. I had to give in.

He peeled the banana for me. As I was eating it, I said, "What a terrible thing it is. It tastes awful! You are spending our good money for stuff like that?"

The train came. It was very pleasant and warm. The train went really fast. Both of us were very quiet. It is a strange feeling when a person does not know their destiny.

Laszlo broke the quiet. "Look, Elizabeth, how beautiful the forest is with the snow."

I answered him, "Yes, it is very beautiful, that Austrian forest." I was wondering what Salzburg would look like. I felt very strange. So far, I had been so fearful that they were going to find my husband and execute him. Now, my feelings were completely different. It seemed to me that we had left our beloved country so long ago—and my mother and the rest of the family. I had a hard time holding my tears back.

I didn't share that feeling with my husband. That man was faithful towards his country. At only sixteen, such a young age, he was already in the war. He must have tortured feelings, too, because we had to leave our home. I truly felt sorry for him.

My husband interrupted my thoughts. "Elizabeth."

I turned to him and said, "What?"

"Aren't you thirsty?"

"Yes, and hungry, too."

"Then I am going to the dining car."

"Bring some sandwiches, too."

At mid-afternoon, we asked the conductor, "When are we going arrive in Salzburg?"

He said, "We will be there by six o'clock."

In the meantime, we ate our sandwiches. It started to get dark. In Vienna, the benches that we slept on were quite hard. I told Laszlo, "I am going to sleep a little bit." Since I love the sound of the train, I fell asleep right away.

I awoke. My husband was gently nudging me. "Elizabeth, we are here!"

I was still half asleep. I asked, "Where? Where?"

"In Salzburg," he answered.

At the train station, we found out which way we should go to the Hungarian refugee camp. We were on our way. The weather was damp and cold.

What a big place. So many refugees. We were lucky. We were not too late for supper. One woman asked us, "Did you just arrive?"

Laszlo said, "Just now."

The woman said she did not think the refugees were still coming. It was already December 13.

Laszlo said, "We left our country on December 12."

She asked, "Was it hard?"

"It took four tries."

"Then I will show you where you will be sleeping. After that, you will get supper."

In the dining hall, we got to know the rest of the people.

Laszlo said we should go to sleep. There were a lot of iron beds divided with white sheets. Our neighbors were a young couple with a baby girl a year-and-a-half old. She cried a lot.

December 14, 1956, was our first day in Salzburg. We were having breakfast, and the woman came up to us. She asked, "Are you going to America?"

Laszlo said, "Yes."

She handed over a lot of documents. "These need to be filled out. Please give them back to me. Then, your medical examination will begin."

She was right: chest x-ray, blood for the lab work, complete examination by a doctor. Six days later, all our documents were in our hands, including a green card. We had no idea how valuable the green cards were. Laszlo suggested we should go out to the city and see how Salzburg looked. I remember, most of all, that the sky was very cloudy. It was very damp and cold. It was not a pleasant place.

We just arrived back at the camp from our city tour. That woman said, "I have been looking for you. Tomorrow morning, you are leaving for Munich. From there, with a plane, you are flying to America."

After supper, we went back to our sleeping quarters. We told the news to the people there. "Tomorrow, we are leaving for Munich." They said they were going, too. We decided we should go to bed. We would have a long day tomorrow and we hoped the baby would sleep more that night.

It wasn't so. In the morning, at breakfast, we also each got a brown bag. They said we should bring them with us on the bus. That would be our lunch. They told us to bring everything else we own. Well, that wasn't a problem, since we didn't have anything else.

It was a nice, pleasant morning. The sun was shining and there was lots of snow on the ground. Five busses were loaded up with people leaving for Munich. We saw the big forest, with lots of snow on the trees; it looked like the enchanted forest.

Ooops! The bus was sliding since the road was snowy and icy. When we arrived in Munich, we were told that we would leave for America the next morning. We received supper at the mess hall, and then were shown where we would be sleeping.

Laszlo said, "I wonder what kind of plane we are going with to America."

I started thinking, *If we are going by plane, then that means America must be very far! When he asked me in Vienna where we should go, I did tell him I didn't care, as long as it was not far. Now we have traveled a whole lot, with the train, with the bus, and now with a plane?* It was looking like we were going very, very, far from Hungary! I started getting mad. *That wasn't the deal,* I thought. *Laszlo is eight years older than I am. He should know more than I do.* I started feeling I was being cheated. Under no circumstances did I want to go far from Mother and Hungary.

My husband said, "Let's go to have supper." It was a big cafeteria with lots of big trays and a bunch of good looking food. Laszlo bragged, "You see, that is American food." There was a translator who said we should eat as much as we liked. There was a lot of fruit and pastry.

I said to Laszlo, "Look at those bananas over there. See how nice and yellow they are? Not like in Vienna; and they are free!"

We enjoyed the dinner. We were familiarizing ourselves with the new tastes. There were all kinds of foods—food we knew, and food we didn't know. It was a tremendous experience.

After supper, they took us to the sleeping quarters. By then, we were very tired. When we were getting ready to go to bed, a man came with a list in his hand. He said, "Those whose name I am going to call, get ready. The plane is waiting. We are leaving for America."

We were very surprised. We said, "We were told we were going in the morning."

The man said, "The plane arrived, and we are leaving in a half an hour."

I was not happy at all. I did not want to go where the plane would take us. It was way too far. Laszlo nervously said, "Come on, Elizabeth, don't be stupid!"

"I told you we can go anywhere, as long as it is not far."

But, my name was on the list. I had to go. We were seated on the plane. It was an old military plane. I thought, *I wonder how far that plane is taking us.* My mother, my twin sister, and my other sisters were in my mind. I started to cry.

Laszlo asked me, "Why are you crying?"

"Because we are going way, way, too far."

He said, "Oh, not at all." He said to me, "Why don't you sleep? You are very tired." I did fall asleep, but not for long. Laszlo turned to me and said, "Aren't you sleeping?"

"I can't. The plane is too noisy."

He also said, "Now, we are crossing over the ocean."

I said, "What kind of ocean?"

He said, "You know, the ocean."

Of course. America is over on the other side of the ocean, I realized. Now I knew we were going really, really, far. I had a very weird feeling. I felt empty. I felt homeless. My throat tightened up. I tried to hold back my tears. How would our life be from now on? I was extremely sad. I don't like changes. I didn't like Budapest, either. It wasn't far. I was able to leave it behind me. And I did. My husband saw how sad I was. He said not to worry.

Chapter 17

December 1956: We Arrived in America

The pilot said we were going to pick up fuel in Nova Scotia. There was a very big snow on the ground. We went into a fairly big room, and there was a young man who had learned Hungarian by singing with his grandfather. The man from Nova Scotia asked the man from the plane, "Would they sing with him?"

In the meantime, Coca-Cola was introduced to us. Oh, it was bad. It was awful. Then they said the plane was ready and we should board it.

We made ourselves comfortable. I said to Laszlo, "I am going to sleep."

I was awakened when Laszlo said, "Here we are!"

Busses came to take us to the military camp—Camp Kilmer. It seemed like it was a long way. Then they showed us where we were going to sleep. They also showed us where we were going to eat. Then they took us into a pretty big room where there were all kinds of clothing: winter coats, shoes, and just everything. I chose a dress. Laszlo chose pants. We walked around, getting to know the place. It was a military camp.

Wow! What were we seeing? Some soldiers had skin that was very black. We started pointing at them. We wanted to make sure everybody saw them. We said, "Did you see how black their skin is?" Their hair was very strange, too.

When we were pointing at them, the loudspeaker started to talk. It said, "Please don't point at the soldiers. You are hurting their feelings." We felt very bad right away. We did not want to hurt anybody's feelings. But, to us, it was an amazing new experience, since we had never seen a Negro person before. After that, we just whispered to each other, "Did you see how black their skin is?"

We went to lunch. We were told there that the head of the family should be at that place at ten in the morning. Business people were coming to take us with them. The next morning, Laszlo left with the rest of the men.

We women anxiously waited for them to return. We really wanted to know where we were going to be taken and when. We were wishing to have a home. Since we had been on the road for two months now, my first word to him was, "What happened?"

He said to me, "You know, it is winter. No one was there who wanted a house painter. But, they said we should be there tomorrow at ten, again."

Very good, we went to lunch. The lunch was good. There were strange tastes, but interesting. On the table was a lot of fruit: apples, oranges, beautiful grapes. We were amazed at such beautiful grapes. In winter time? Well, that is America. That was a very different world. The food was plentiful.

After lunch, we went back to the warehouse where the clothes were. Laszlo really needed a pair of shoes since the sole was coming down on the pair he had on. Since his feet were size 13, he couldn't find a pair of shoes. He found rubber boots. Since I was looking in the girls department, he came to me. He said very proudly, "Look what I found."

I said, "Those are rubber boots. Your feet will freeze in them. Where are your shoes?"

He said, "I left them back there."

"We should go, right away, and try to find them before somebody takes them." We were very lucky. Since they were size 13, not many men have that big a foot. So, we found them. We also found a lining for the rubber boots.

"Now, you will be all right for a while."

It would be nice to have a rest before supper. We went back to our sleeping quarters. Again, we had nice, white sheets for privacy walls, just like in Salzburg. We were restless. We would like to have a home already.

Finally, we fell asleep. After our rest, Laszlo said, "Let's go for supper."

It was already five-thirty, and it was almost completely dark. The days were short. We hoped we wouldn't have to be here very long. As we went to the cafeteria, Laszlo said, "I hope somebody is going to take us tomorrow. I haven't worked in two months. And I wonder where we will wind up, in this big country. You know, tomorrow is December 28. Yes, pretty soon it will be New Year."

I said, "Do you know what a weird feeling it is to be a refugee?"

My husband said, "Yes." He also said, "I can't wait until morning. I will be at that place at nine in the morning."

I said, "Don't you have to be there at ten?"

"Yes, but I don't want anybody to miss me."

"All right, as you wish."

At the cafeteria, there were a lot of people. On their faces, fatigue and worry showed through. We were just realizing we didn't speak that language. So far, it hadn't mattered until now. Now we were here, and they spoke English. It is a very serious problem, not understanding what people are saying. That was bad. My husband said, "Don't get yourself upset. You won't be able to sleep."

"Yes, you are right. We will learn it."

After supper, we went back into our sleeping quarters. Before falling asleep, we talked, wondering what was happening at home. We didn't know any news. We were already feeling the language barrier. It seemed to us we were an island, just the two of us—since we were only able to understand each other's voice.

I realized my husband was already asleep. I lay thinking a while longer. *My poor mother, she must be crying after me. Anna has a baby. I wonder if she is very sad that I am not there. I am not able to see what she got. I would love to be there and help her. We would take the baby in the baby carriage for a walk. Everyone should be able to see what Anna has. Since everybody knows each other, I am sure we would stop every ten feet so they can see the little baby Zsa Zsa. Oh, I miss them so! I wonder when I will be able to see them and my little country. I had better go to sleep. I am so homesick! That hurts. That is dif-*

ferent from when I was in Budapest. Here I can't see my way out of this. Here, there is a big ocean between us. I don't want to think any more.

I knew I had better go to sleep, but I was wide awake. *Why did I get into this situation? I never wished to see the world. Destiny has been rude to me. But, I wonder why? This is not a joke.* I told myself my husband would not have been able to get out of the country without me. I was the one who found the three young Jewish couples on the train. I'm the one who said, "Let's hitch ourselves to them." Without them, we would not have been able to get out of the country. Yes, that is how my husband's life was saved. Now I had better go to sleep. I wondered what tomorrow will bring.

My husband called my name. "Elizabeth, wake up. We have to go have breakfast. You know I have to go to the office at ten."

I was half asleep. I said, "Yes. Yes."

He said, "I very much hope someone will take us today." After breakfast, we walked into the camp. It was not too cold. The camp was so quiet. We could see a few soldiers coming and going. That is probably because it is between Christmas and New Years.

On December 28, we were done with breakfast, and my husband said goodbye. He went to the office. That is where they met the business people. I went to the warehouse where the clothes were kept. I thought, *I am going to find myself a couple of dresses. Who knows when we will have money to buy?* (Note to the reader: On this book's cover there is a picture where I am wearing one of these dresses.) Pretty, isn't it? I had them a long time until I outgrew them.

One hour later, my husband came looking for me. He said, "Let's go to lunch. I need to go back there in the afternoon."

Then I asked, "Then there is no one to take us yet?"

My husband said, "I am sorry. No. Maybe there will be in the afternoon."

There were fewer people in the cafeteria. One couple said, "We will be taken to North Carolina." The other said, "We are going to Chicago." Somebody else said, "We are going to Washington." Someone else said, "We will be taken to Maryland." "We are going to Detroit." "We are going to Ohio." "We are going to Pittsburgh." "We will be taken to Texas." "We are going to New Jersey." A man said, "I am going to New York. I am a chef." "We are to be taken to Virginia." These people were very happy. At the same time, they were worried about the unknown. It is a bad feeling not to know where you are going. I thought, *My dear God, how we will be spread around in that big country!*

After lunch, my husband went back to the office. He said to me, "As soon as I know anything, I will come." In the meantime, I walked around, looking around. I wanted time to pass. I went back to the sleeping quarters, as it was warmer there. At four in the afternoon, my husband came running. He said, "We are going to Alexandria."

"Wow! I wonder where that is."

He said, "It is near to Washington." Laszlo said, "He is an older gentleman and his name is Mr. Baldi. He is the one who is taking us and the Gazdag's."

"Who are they? The other family?"

"He is an electrician. They have a seven-year-old little boy. Mr. Baldi has a big apartment project and also a big hotel in Washington. We are leaving shortly." My husband was happy, and I was, too.

But also, it was in my thoughts that we were still going further.

We went to the car. It was a big black Cadillac. The Gazdag family was already standing there, with four big bags of clothes. We had a small bag. Mr. Baldi asked, "Where is the rest of your stuff?"

Laszlo said, "That is all. The people who still come, they will need clothes, too. All we took was what we needed."

Mr. Baldi right away said, "What a difference between the two families." The bags were put into the trunk of the car. Mr. Baldi said, "Since Laszlo is tall, he should sit in the front. Mr. Baldi had a big cigar in his mouth. I thought, *I hope he is not going to come into that car with the big cigar, because I am going to choke to death.*

Mr. Baldi sat in the car with that tremendous cigar in his mouth. We were on our way. Right away, my stomach turned upside down. I started to pray. I was hoping Mr. Baldi would finish that cigar very soon. I looked at the cigar. I noticed that there was not much left. I thought, *Thank God!* The next minute, he had a new cigar in his hand and he was lighting it from the old one. If I would have dared to scream in my agony, I would have shouted, "No! No!" I didn't know what to do.

There was snow on the ground and the car was going slowly. I was asking Laszlo if he had any idea how far was Alexandria. Of course, he did not know. He said, "You will find out when we get there." I thought, *No matter how far it is I will not survive that anyway. I am so nauseated.*

The car stopped. On the building, it said Howard Johnson. Mr. Baldi motioned that we were going to go in. We sat in the dining room. The waitress brought us the menu and she waited for us to order. Mr. Baldi looked at us. We looked at him. Right away, he came to the conclusion that he was the one who had to order the supper.

In the meantime, we noticed the table next to us. A Negro family was sitting with a little boy about five years old. When the Gazdag family's little boy saw him, he looked at the little boy's curly hair and dark skin. He stood in front of the little boy and was touching the top of the little boy's head. The Hungarian mother said, "No, John, no! Come back here. Come on to eat."

Mr. Baldi paid and then motioned that we were leaving. Oh, my God! Already a big, big, cigar was in his mouth!

As we got into the car, I made sure I did not sit behind Mr. Baldi. But, that didn't help. The horrible cigar smell and the smoke floated in the car everywhere.

Chapter 18

December 28, 1956: Our New Alexandria Home

At nine in the evening, we stopped in front of the big apartment project. Mr. Baldi motioned to get out of the car. There was a man with keys in his hands. He led the Gazdag family into their future home. We sat back into the car. Forty minutes later, we stopped in front of a hotel in Washington, D.C. Mr. Baldi took us into the hotel room and he showed us on his watch; in the morning, he would come and pick us up.

I could not thank God enough. We were able to close the door behind him. I told my husband quickly, "I am going to take a shower."

He said to me, "It is midnight. You are going to wake up the neighbors."

I insisted. "But I must take a shower. Every inch of me smells like a cigar. I promise I will hurry."

Morning came fast and Mr. Baldi would be there shortly to pick us up. Mr. Baldi picked us up and then the Gazdog family, also. He then took us some place for breakfast. After breakfast, Mr. Baldi took us furniture shopping: bedroom suite, kitchen table and four chairs, silverware, china. The china had a flowery design on it and also some other design. He told us, since we were the ladies in the house, we should choose the pattern of the china. When that was all done, he also took us grocery shopping in the Giant food store. Mr. Baldi gave me twenty dollars, and the same amount to Rozsa (Mrs. Gazdog), too. He also showed us how to push the shopping cart. Then he came along with us. The grocery store had everything you can imagine, but we had no idea what the twenty dollars was worth. Therefore, we were afraid to touch anything.

Mr. Baldi started putting the milk, butter, bread, coffee . . . when he put the chicken into the cart Gazdog Rozsa fell into a panic. She turned to me and she said, "You see what he is doing? The coffee must weigh a half a kilo and a whole chicken? What is that man thinking? How are we going to pay for all of that?"

Maybe from the twenty dollars he gave us?" I said to her. "We don't need to be in a panic. He knows what he gave us."

When we got to the cashier's, we were waiting nervously to find how much we had to pay. The Gazdog family paid eleven dollars and some cents. We paid nine dollars and some cents. Very surprised, we looked at each other. Well, it seemed like that dollar was worth a whole lot. Rozsa was all relaxed then.

We dropped the Gazdog family at the end of Florence Drive. That is where they have a two-bedroom apartment. At the beginning of Florence Drive, the car stopped again and we followed Mr. Baldi. We were going to live here in a one bedroom apartment in the basement, next to the laundry room and the trash room. The black man was there with the keys. He opened the door. In the kitchen, there was the kitchen table with four chairs. Mr. Baldi showed us the rest of the apartment, the bedroom. The bedroom furniture was in it. We were amazed how fast it came here from the furniture store. In the living room, there was a big, dark red couch. In the kitchen, a pretty, big, green refrigerator, and a stove with four burners. I thought, *That is something.*

Mr. Baldi said goodbye and left. Soon after that, a man came, and took Laszlo with him. About a half hour later, Laszlo came back. I was anxious, and asked, "Where did the man take you?"

Laszlo said, "At the end of the building is a room. That is where all of the painting tools and paint are.

"I am going to paint that apartment project. The other street called Milan Drive is a part of the project, too. Altogether about six hundred apartments are here."

We looked at each other. We had nothing to unpack. What should we do now? We decided we should go to see the Gazdog family.

They were very happy when they saw us. They didn't know what to do either. In the conversation, we found out how much who gets paid. Laszlo got two hundred dollars a month and that one-bedroom apartment. He had to work six days a week. Mr. Gazdog John also was paid two hundred dollars a month, and that two-bedroom apartment. Rozsa said that was not fair, since they had a child. We said we did not decide who gets paid how much.

We sensed jealousy. I said to Laszlo, "Let's go home and bake that chicken."

Since the next day was New Year's Day, at home we already were dancing. We felt ourselves alone. My husband said, "I am going to work tomorrow."

I said, "Where would you go to work tomorrow? Don't you know tomorrow is New Years Day?"

"Yes, I know. But the superintendent showed me what I am going to paint."

"What are you going to paint?" I began arguing.

"If you must know . . ."

"Yes, of course, I want to know."

"Very well. You remember the iron fence before we turn into that apartment project?"

"Yes, I thought it was nice." I argued. "Don't tell me that is what you are going to paint! Those are outside. And it is winter. And they are made out of iron. You are going to catch cold."

Laszlo said, "They told me that is what I should do, and that is what I have to do."

I argued further. "What kind of country is this America? I thought New Year's is a holiday everywhere in the world. I am very shocked they are not celebrating New Year's in America."

He said, "I am sorry."

"But I don't want to stay here alone."

"But I am not going anywhere now. Why don't you bake the chicken? I am hungry."

Now, we had to find out how that oven worked. It was written on it. Too bad we didn't read English. My husband said, "We will learn it!" In the meantime, we pushed the buttons. Poof! We got it! The oven was on. We could bake the chicken.

We were done with the dinner, and I said, "Let's go for a walk."

Laszlo said, "Good idea! It is not dark yet."

We were absolutely shocked. We didn't see a soul anywhere! In Sztalinvaros, the streets were full of people all of the time. We wondered where the people were. We found the Giant grocery store where we bought the groceries earlier. We thought, *Very good. It is not too far.*

It was cold and we went back to the apartment. It was nice and warm in our apartment. We had a small dictionary. We were reading it. I saw my husband was worried. I said, "Don't worry Laszlo. In six months, we will speak English very well."

"All right, but now let's go to bed. We should try out our new bed."

In the morning, January 1, 1957, my husband dressed in the white painter's pants they gave him.

I said to him, "I don't want to stay here alone."

He said, "Later on, when it warms up, come on out where the fence is."

"All right, but I don't like to be here alone."

"I understand," he said. "I am sorry." He kissed me and he left.

I had nothing to do. The apartment was quite dark, since it was a basement apartment. It did have windows in it. I went from one window to another. Absolutely nowhere was there a soul. At home, when I looked out from the window, I always saw people coming and going on the street. I wondered what Mother and everyone were doing. Oh, I missed them so much. We had to write to them right away since we now had an address. Poor Mother, I was sure she was very worried about us. My eyes filled up with tears. I didn't want to cry. I was a big girl.

Somebody knocked on the door. "Who is it?" I yelled.

My husband said, "It is I." I let him in.

"What happened?" I asked. "You would be pleased to know New Year's is a holiday in the United States, too!"

I was very happy. "How did you find out?"

He started explaining, "I am standing and painting the iron fence. A window opened. She started talking to me in English. She realized I didn't understand her. She said 'Sprechen sie Deutsch?' I said to her 'Ja!' Then she came out of the apartment. She said to me 'You come with me.' We went to the office. She asked the superintendent, 'Why is that man painting the iron fence on New Year's Day?' The superintendent was very ashamed of himself. Then he said, 'Please tell Mr. Dobosi to go home to his wife.'"

Then my husband told me, "We are invited this afternoon for cookies and coffee."

That is how we met Trudi and Mooney on January 1, 1957. They were our very first American friends.

After living in Alexandria for three days, I got a letter on its way to Mother. In the evening, there was a knock on the door. We looked at each other. *Who could that be?* We opened the door. Three couples were standing at the door. We invited them in.

We found the dictionary right away. We found out they were our neighbors. They lived above us. Betty Davis, and Don, her husband; Jo Ann. Margaret, she lived on the first floor. They had a candy dish. They said they brought it for the boy. We explained that we don't have any children. The other couple had the little boy. It seemed like they understood what we were showing from the dictionary. We were very happy for our new neighbors.

Laszlo worked painting the apartments. He had not been sent out since to paint the iron fence. Rozsa and I got to know each other. Zoli, their little boy, went to school.

Rozsa and I went to the Giant every day. That is what we were used to. Fresh bread every day. We bought our food that we were going to cook for supper. Before we went to the cashier, we pretty much figured out how much we were going to pay. We didn't understand why the smaller money was worth more than the bigger one, for instance, the dime and the nickel. We put them in our hands and let the cashier take out what she needed.

We did that every day till Rozsa got a job washing dishes in the hospital. I was alone, again. Most of my time I spent on that big, old, dark red couch, with my little dictionary. Shortly, I realized that the English language could not be read like the Hungarian language. This would be much harder than I had thought. Probably it would take longer than six months for us to learn English.

Chapter 19

February 1957: Attempted Rape

We had been three weeks living in America. I was reading the dictionary. Somebody knocked on the door. I opened the door, thinking it might be my husband. A Negro man was standing in the door and started pushing me in. We were near that big, dark red couch. He forcefully pushed me down. I was shocked. I jumped up, ran to the door. I opened the door. I yelled at him, "Get out! Get out!" He left.

I started crying. I didn't know which apartment Laszlo was painting. I went out to the street. I didn't see anyone. I was waiting very much for Laszlo to come home. I stood on the sidewalk. I could see the end of the street. Laszlo was coming. I started running toward him.

He said, "Hello. Is the supper ready?"

I told him, "I didn't cook." I started telling him, "I almost got raped!"

He asked "Who?"

I told him, "A black man."

We decided that, the next morning when the office opened, we would report it. Shortly after we got home, the Gazdogs came over. We told them what happened. They looked at each other.

We said, "What? What is going on?"

They said, "Yesterday, a man tried to rape Rozsa."

We were very sorry. We asked them, "Did you report him?"

They reluctantly said "No."

We told them, "You have to report him. In the morning when the office opens, we are going to report him, and you should, too. If not, we are going to have to worry that he will come back."

The next morning in the office, Miss Baldi was very surprised. She promised she would take care of the problem. In the evening, we were sitting at the dinner table. There was a knock on the door.

Laszlo opened the door. There were two policemen. They asked me, "Is he the one?"

I said, "Yes! He is the one."

Then they went to Rozsa's apartment. She identified him, too. He was the one.

The next day, the translator came. She informed us that we would have to appear in court in front of the judge and identify the man who wanted to rape us. On the designated date, the translator would come and pick us up. We agreed to it.

In the court, the judge asked the man, "Why did you go to the two refugee women?" His answer was that, since he was in the military, he had had women from most of the countries, but he had not had any Hungarian women.

I don't remember his punishment, but we hoped we would not have that kind of problem again.

I went to the grocery store by myself, since Rozsa was working. I thought, *Oh, it would be so nice it I had a job too!" Oh, I am so lonely. I miss Mother. I miss my twin sister, friends, the Dozsa movie theater, Steel Mill Street.* There were always a lot of people on that street. It did not matter where I looked here, I couldn't see anyone, anywhere! My homesickness was stronger every day. I was hurting. I didn't like it here. A thought came into my mind, *I'm going to close my eyes and, when I open them again, I will be back home, because this is just a dream, a very bad dream.* When I opened my eyes, I was still standing in that basement apartment in the kitchen in front of the window. My throat got tight. My tears poured down on my face. *How long will we have to be here? When are we going home? That is why I didn't want to go too far. As soon as possible, we are going home.*

Trudi and Mooney came over for a short visit. We stared at each other. From the little dictionary, you can't have a lively conversation. Trudi brought over a bed spread and two towels. We needed them.

After about four weeks, Trudi and Mooney asked us over to watch TV. We happily accepted the invitation.

After watching the TV, we decided we would have to buy a TV as soon as possible. I said to my husband, "It would be a good tool to learn English. At the same time, it is very entertaining." He thought so, too. We started to put money away for the TV. Of course, from the two hundred dollars Laszlo got, we had to have the plane ticket cost taken out. Then the bed room suite, kitchen table, and dishes, but we were going to save wherever possible.

Laszlo told me he ran into John Gazdog. John said, "There is a school to learn English. It costs five dollars per month, per person." And they decided the two of them were going.

I asked, "What about us girls?"

"Well, you know we can't afford both of us. Since we are the men of the household, I think John and I should go." Reluctantly, I agreed to it.

The days were slow and long. I was thinking more and more about home. My homesickness was tremendous., I was crying every day. I remembered the boy who thought I was his girl friend, When I told him, "I'm sorry, but I thought we were just friends," he said to me, "You just wait. You will cry when nobody sees you." I realized what that boy had said to me. He had cursed me! I was crying. And, no one saw me—just like he said.

Chapter 20

July 1957: My First Job in America

When we had been living in Dominion Gardens for seven months, Trudi came running to our place and told me, with both hands, that she had got a job for me! I was so happy. I was hugging her and hugging her.

That was the fourth miracle!

Trudi was working in Alexandria in a Venetian blind factory. She was making ninety cents per hour. Coca-Cola offered her an extra five cents. Trudi talked it over with Martin in the shade shop. She told him he should hire me. I would be able to do that since that work did not require any language skill. Since Martin was a very good and kind man, he told Trudi to bring me over. She introduced me to Martin and she left.

It was a long, warehouse-type building. There were eight women, Martin, the boss, Billy, and Ron. Martin told me to do what the rest of them were doing. As I watched what they were doing, I said to myself, *That is very good. That job doesn't really require any language skill.* At lunch time, they were having lunch, and watching me. When they realized I was feeling uncomfortable, they tried to explain to me they were very sorry. The reason they were looking at me is because I was very pretty.

Rita was a German girl, just like Trudi, married to an American soldier. Rita bought me a bottle of Coca-Cola out of the machine. She explained she was going to take me home after work since she lived at the same place. And in the mornings, I could come to work with them.

My husband was anxiously waiting to see me that night. I had to tell him about the whole day. He was happy because I was happy.

The next week there was a payday. I was very happy to go to work. I was crying less. Payday! I received, for a week's pay, thirty-one dollars and some cents. Laszlo and I decided my paycheck would be enough for the food and household expenses. We would be able to save more out of his paycheck, and shortly we will be able to buy a TV. And we would be able to send packages to home.

Mother said in her letter that she never thought we would go so far away. The situation was bad at home. We should send clothes to the girls. I would send Anna lots of baby clothes, pretty little dresses. She needed them, since Zsa Zsa was a year old.

I liked to go to work. Everyone was teaching me English. I liked these people. Martin was a very good man.

John and Laszlo were going to English school. Laszlo was working, too. He liked the fact you didn't have to mix the paint; you just had to open the can and paint. That roller was very good. You could accomplish so much more than with a brush.

Very soon, it would be a year we had been in America. We could not brag with our English skill. I did tell Laszlo, "Not to worry. In six months we will be speaking English."

We were trying. We were going to buy a TV. Christmas would be here shortly. The package to Mother was on its way: a big one. Anna's package would be there shortly. The next project was to save money to buy a car!

Martin from work was having a Christmas party at his house. Laszlo bought me a party dress. It had no sleeves; not even straps on my shoulders. All night, I worried that the dress would slide down to my stomach and my breasts would fall out. When the party was over, no shame had come to us.

At home, everybody was at Mother's house. Mother cooked her special stuffed cabbage and pastries. On that special day, we were always very happy to go home. On the trains, it was terribly crowded. We stood like sardines in a sardine box; but it was always worth it to make the trip. Mother and Father were very happy. All their children were under their roof. I'm sure Mother was missing us.

I thought, *Oh! How I would love to see them! I should write a letter to Mother.* No matter how many times I sat down, paper and pen in my hands, I couldn't write it. What could I write? My throat would be tight. My eyes were full of tears. *Should I write that I don't like to be here? That I am very homesick, and I am crying a lot?* I couldn't write these things down.

Mother would be terribly upset. I was sure she would write back to me, "Come home, my little girl!" How could I go home? Since I left the country illegally, I would be punished. Until the regime changed, we could not go home. I decided I would not write right away. I would write some other time.

At home, the whole city was Laszlo's friend. He didn't complain, but he showed the loneliness and the homesickness. His mother wrote. She said in her letter that a lot of people from Baja, where Laszlo is from, were living in New Jersey. Laszlo said, "We need a car." We were going to save money for it.

Easter was coming. Betty and Don took us to his parents' house. It was a big family. On Easter Monday, we would go to work. At home, that is a big holiday. Boys and men go to houses with a perfume bottle. They visit every woman they know and, with a pretty poem, they sprinkle perfume on the women, like when you are watering the flowers so they won't wilt. That is a very nice tradition. For appreciation, the boys are offered money and red eggs. The men are offered wine and liquor. By the time they had visited every friend and neighbor, the poor men were really drunk.

Since everybody walked, it really wasn't a problem.

Our money was coming together nicely. It looked like we would be able to buy a car in the fall.

Joe Ann said, "We are going to Ocean City. Would you like to go with us?" They had room in their car for us. The other two neighbors were coming, too. Right away, we decided who would make the potato salad and Cole slaw. It was my job to make the fried chicken.

It was a tremendous experience, seeing the magnificent ocean. Laszlo went into the ocean. A huge wave came and threw him right back out to the shore. He lost the skin off both his knees. He came to realize in a hurry what energy a wave like that has. We enjoyed the potato salad and Cole slaw. Every one raved about my fried chicken. They said I should sell the recipe.

We got home exhausted, but had a very good time.

We had a problem. Trudi and Rita got into an argument. It was childish. Since I was riding with Rita to work and the argument was about me, Rita told me I could not ride with them to work in the mornings any more. She said I could let Trudi take me to work.

Now we really needed a car. For the next month, Trudi devotedly took me to work every morning. And I took the bus home in the afternoon. One afternoon, I saw my bus coming. I started running. I guess the driver didn't see me. He pulled out of the bus station without me. A young man saw that. He stopped the car next to me. He tried to tell me he saw me miss the bus. He would be glad to take me home. I tried to explain to him that he didn't have to. But, he stood there with his car and insisted he would like very much to take me home. In the meantime, I thought, *I have to wait another half hour until the next bus and it is so very hot.* When I finished that thought, I told him okay. I thought, *I am going to go into the Giant grocery store and I am going to send him away.* When we got to the Giant, I said, "Thank you very much. Goodbye."

He explained to me that he was going to wait for me. I thanked him again and tried to explain he should not wait for me. I was in the store and tried to see if he had left. But, he was still there, sitting in the car in the parking lot. I thought, *I should be home cooking dinner. I can't stay here in this store forever. I have no choice. I have to come out.* When he saw me coming, he opened the car door right away.

So then, I had another thought. Since we lived in Florence Drive, I would have him deliver me to Milan Drive and tell him that was where I lived. I didn't want him to know where I lived. I thanked him very much for the ride and told him, "Goodbye, goodbye." As soon as he pulled away on the road, I ran home, since I was late cooking dinner.

During dinner, my husband asked me if I came home on a bus.

I said "Yes. Yes."

The next day I came home on the bus. I cooked the dinner. I started wondering. My husband should be home by now.

Oh, finally he arrived! I asked him, "Where have you been?" I could see he was very upset.

He asked me angrily, "How did you come home?"

I told him I took the bus.

He said to me, angrily, "You are lying! I saw you yesterday on Milan Drive with some young man with a nice convertible car. You were getting out of it."

Of course, right away, he thought the worst of it. Today he was standing with a baseball bat and he said, "I was waiting for you guys."

I said to him, "Oh, that is the way you are spending your time! And the dinner is getting cold." I explained to him what had happened. Finally, he calmed down. I said to him, "When we have a car, you are the one who will take me to work and everywhere."

He asked, "How are we doing with the money?"

"By October, we will be able to buy a car."

Like an inexperienced car buyer, we purchased a 1957 Chevrolet: four-door, two-tone, white and green. It was a lemon! Trudi and Mooney taught Laszlo how to drive. Then we went to Alexandria to the Bureau of Motor Vehicles for Laszlo to take the driving test out of the dictionary. Well, Laszlo received a driving license. The four of us were jumping up and down with happiness.

Then we heard about the Hungarian Club in Washington, D.C. We met Horvath Laszlo, who became our very good friend, and others. We also found out Hungarians lived in New Jersey. Among them were butchers from Baja. New Jersey was where we were going the next weekend. We told the news to our neighbors. They said to us, "We don't speak English. How would we dare to go so far?"

We told them, "With a map."

In New Jersey, we found out a lot of butchers were working in New York. The butchers from Baja were known everywhere for the wonderful sausage and bacon they made. It was a wonderful experience seeing New

York. Laszlo was very happy to see his home town people and friends. And they promised they would come to Virginia to visit us.

Chapter 21

1959: Surgery is Necessary

In 1959, many times I woke up during the night. My stomach hurt a lot. I told Trudi that I was sick just about every single night.

Trudi knew a friend who had a Hungarian doctor, and they gave the telephone number and address to us. Trudi said, "Go see that doctor. He is a good doctor."

One horrible night, we decided to be at the doctor's office as soon as he opened. He laid me down on a table and examined my stomach. He said, "I think you have a gall stone. You need to have an x-ray taken to be sure."

Well, the diagnosis was correct. I needed surgery. Now we were worried we would have to save up the money for the surgery. Six months later, we had the money saved up. It was just about time, because I was in very bad shape. All I dared to eat was toast. I was very skinny.

On September 10, 1959, I was in a Washington hospital. I was over the surgery. Dr. Tober Laszlo, Dr. Gondor Laszlo's friend, did the surgery, but just in time, because my gall bladder was infected. I would not have lived long without the surgery.

I began feeling better. I even asked the doctor to let me go home. He said that, when I was able to walk across the room, he would let me go home. It wasn't easy, since my stomach had a very long cut on it. But I mustered up all of my strength and made it across the room. Eight days seemed very long. I was eager to be home.

Laszlo came to take me home. We were very happy. When we stood at the counter to pay for my surgery, the secretary said, "It is already paid for." We were very surprised. Martin was there. The secretary said, "He paid for it!" I said before, he was a wonderful man. Dr. Tober was a good surgeon. I started feeling like I was reborn.

Three weeks after my surgery, I was ready to go back to work. I was also very sexy. My husband was happy and so was I.

Since Mooney was in the military, he had to go to Korea. We were hoping no harm came to him.

On that weekend, we were having company from New Jersey—Laszlo's home town friends. Physically, I felt better every day. But, the homesickness still made me cry often. I missed Mother and everyone very much.

My husband and I talked. Maybe, if we had children, it would be better. We wouldn't be so lonely. We started thinking how happy we would be if I would get pregnant.

We were getting ready to go to the Christmas party and New Year's party with Betty Davis. We were going to the Police Ball. Finally, all of the parties were over.

Everybody was going back to work. In January 1960, a big snow fell on the ground during the night. In the morning, the people were going to work, but they were stuck in the parking lot, in the snow. Laszlo helped push everyone out of the parking lot. My husband was young, strong, a wrestling champion, and very handsome.

We planned to see Dr. Gondor the next week. We wanted to find out if I were pregnant. We couldn't wait. We were progressing with our English language.

We called all of our friends together. We wanted to share with them our very happy news. Dr. Gondor said I was pregnant! My husband and I were very happy. The only problem was that my stomach was very sick every morning. Dr. Gondor said that would stop.

Oh, but I really hoped so. I remembered when Mother was pregnant. She was very sick, too. Poor Mother, she was pregnant twelve times! But, we only wanted to have two children.

Now, we would have to write the happy news to Mother right away.

At the end of March, in Washington, D.C., the cherry blossoms were blooming everywhere. Laszlo said, "Let's go see them." It was a very good idea. When I got dressed, my husband asked, "Where is the pregnant dress that we bought last week?"

I told him, "It is too soon yet."

"Put your pregnant dress on, please."

"But," I insisted, "my stomach is not big enough yet."

He didn't want to leave the house until I put my pregnant dress on. So, I put on my pregnant dress. My husband said, "I am so proud of you!" He also said, "A pregnant woman is so beautiful!"

At my workplace, the only thing that changed was that I stood next to the table and put the string into the Venetian blinds, so I didn't have to bend down.

When I was seven months pregnant, Laszlo became worried that something might go wrong, and he thought I should stay home. I had to agree to it. I told them at work that Laszlo wanted me to stay home. My coworkers and Martin were unhappy that I was not coming to work anymore. I told them that I would miss them tremendously. And it was so. I became very lonely again.

I went to shop for baby clothes. We bought a baby bed. We were all ready; now we were just waiting.

One Sunday morning when we woke up, I told my husband that was not the same kind of morning as the others.

He got very excited. "How is it, how is it? Tell me. Does it hurt?"

"Not too much."

"Let's call the doctor."

"Not yet."

"Let me know."

"I will, I will let you know."

On Sunday afternoon, he watched every move I made. At ten o'clock Sunday night, I told Laszlo, "Now, that is not a joke."

He called Dr. Gondor. The doctor asked, "How is the pain?" He said, "It is not time to go to the hospital yet. But, if a change comes, you should call me back." He told us we should go to bed.

About a half hour passed. I told my husband, "The change is here. Doctor said to go to the hospital."

Chapter 22

September 26, 1960: Little Laszlo is Born

We got to the Alexandria hospital by twelve-thirty, September 26, 1960. In the morning, junior Laszlo Dobosi was born; four kilo, fifty-five centimeters long (eight pounds, twelve ounces, twenty-one inches long). A beautiful baby! Oh, we were so happy for him.

His father said, "That baby is so big, next week he can go to kindergarten! But, let him stay home for a while."

The baby and I stayed six days in the hospital. There were six of us in the room of new mothers. But, I was the only one who breast fed the baby. We were so happy to have the baby! So far, there had just been the two of us; but now we were family.

It was completely different. You can't compare it. We decided right away when our little boy was a year old, we were going to order from the stork a baby girl. I got to know Nellie. She was from England. She had an American husband: Harold. We became good friends. Nellie didn't work, therefore, she spent most of her days with us.

I told Laszlo we were going to have a birthday party for the baby. He was a year old. Therefore, we could write an order sheet for the stork. We were ready for a baby girl. A short time later, we got the message that in nine months we would receive a baby girl: Victoria.

My husband was going to get a hair cut. He asked, "Can I take Junior with me? About an hour later, the door opened, and there stood my bald-headed little boy! I couldn't believe my eyes! He is all bald. Where was his beautiful golden blond hair I so admired?

I was very mad. And my husband knew it. I told him it would be best for him to not come in the house. We overcame that.

I told Laszlo he should ask for a two-bedroom apartment so the children would have their own bedroom. The next day he came home. He told me, "Guess what? We are going to move into a bigger apartment."

I asked him "Where?"

He said, "Across the street."

We were very happy for the bigger apartment. And, it was nice and sunny, not like that basement apartment. I told my husband, "Now you have been working for Mr. Baldi for five and a half years. They don't give a raise, they don't give a vacation, and no hospitalization. Five and a half years, and they still pay you only two hundred dollars. Six days a week," I said. "That is not fair!"

He said "But, that is all they give."

"Then you have to go to work somewhere else."

The next day, I told Natalie that Laszlo was mad. She asked, "Why?"

"I told him he has to go to work some place else. That money is not enough, even though I am very careful with the money."

Natalie said, "Harold is a house painter, too. And he works for Mr. Brown, at the Brown Company. Harold could take Laszlo and introduce him to Mr. Brown."

Laszlo reluctantly agreed to it. Mr. Brown liked Laszlo right away. He said, "Laszlo, you are hired."

He thanked him for the job. He said, "I must give two weeks notice to Mr. Baldi."

The next day, in the office, he told of his intention. Mr. Baldi's daughter got very mad. Laszlo said, "We would like to live here and pay rent."

Ms. Baldi said, "Absolutely not! If you are not working here, you will move out right away." She behaved very badly. Laszlo was very worried. What were we going to do?

I told him not to worry, that I would take care of it.

The next day I went into the office. I told Ms. Baldi, "The end of next month I am going to have a baby. Right now, we are not moving anywhere. When the baby is born, and I feel well, then we are going to move. In the meantime, we are going to pay the rent." Then I told her Laszlo should not have been working here six days a week, not a day's vacation, for two hundred dollars a month." That was very unfair for so long!

The next day, Ms. Baldi sent her secretary to me. She said, "Ms. Baldi is very sorry and you should stay here as long as you like to."

Chapter 23

June 29, 1962: Victoria is Born

On June 29, 1962, we got up in the morning at the usual time, about six. I made my husband a sandwich for lunch. When he was leaving, he said to me, "Good luck." I thought that was strange.

At 7:00 AM, I had my first labor pain. That was mighty powerful. I didn't know where Laszlo was working, since they were working in different places.

I called Natalie on the telephone. I told her the baby was coming. She said, "I will be right over."

I called my doctor. I told him how strong my labor pains were. He told me to go to the hospital. One of the neighbor men took me to the Alexandria hospital. Nellie watched over little Laszlo. It was 12:30 PM when our little baby girl was born. Six pounds, twelve ounces, twenty inches, with long, black hair.

Our neighbors decorated our entrance door. They wrote out on ribbons, "The baby girl is born!" And they stood on the sidewalk—right where we live. They wanted to see Laszlo's reaction when he got home.

When he read the ribbon saying we had a girl, he jumped way high up and threw his hat way high. He right away went into the apartment. He gave his cigars to the neighbors. In the meantime, they already bought a bouquet of flowers which they put in his hands.

When he came into my room, he said, "I saw our baby girl. She is beautiful!"

I asked him, "Why didn't you change your clothes?"

He looked at himself. He said, "I didn't realize."

We were very happy. A little boy, a pretty little girl, and they were healthy, too. I told my husband, "We will be in the hospital for three days with Victoria. Nellie is watching little Laszlo during the day while you are working. Again, I am the only one who is breast feeding the baby." I thought, *Too bad.*

We came home from the hospital and little Laszlo was very happy. In three days, he was speaking British English! I looked at Nellie and said, "What is that?" She was very proud of herself.

My husband was working in his new place. It was very good that he was not by himself. He also brought home a pay check. Instead of two hundred dollars, he brought home a paycheck of four hundred and fifty dollars!

Our life was nice. Since we had two little kids, there was less time to worry about homesickness. But, I was very sad that Mother and the rest of them couldn't see my little babies. And I missed the advice, too.

Next month we were going to move to the Donnelly apartments. Two bedrooms, first floor. It had a swimming pool, a very, very nice apartment project. But we would miss our neighbors.

On the first of September, 1962, we moved. "Moving up," like the Jefferson's say. Lots of young couples lived here, just like us, with little children. I could see it would be good to live here. Our neighbors, Beverly, Doris, Margaret, and the rest, seemed like nice people.

Nellie came often. She would spend the day with us. I put milk in her tea, just like in my coffee. We were saving nicely out of Laszlo's new job.

At the end of January 1963, the painting really slowed down. Not to worry, Mr. Brown bid on a big government job. If it came through, it would be a lot of work.

It was the end of February, there was still no work. Mr. Brown didn't get the government job. He was out-bid. Howard and Laszlo went all over in northern Virginia and tried to find work.

At the beginning of March, Howard and Laszlo went again to find work. They found a couple of days work.

On March 15, my husband came home without work. He said to me, "Elizabeth, please sit down, I want to talk to you."

I thought it must be very important. "All right, I am all ears."

"Now almost a month and a half I have hardly worked." He said. "I think I am going to start working for myself."

I said "But then, you have to buy a truck."

My husband said, "In the meantime, the car will do. I am going to take out the back seat. I am going to put the tools there. What do you think?" he asked me.

"Very good, if you think so, too."

March 15 is a Hungarian holiday. In 1848, March 15, it was the first Hungarian Revolution. Petofi Sandor, the poet, wrote:

National Song
Rise up, Magyar, the country calls!
It's "now or never" what fate befalls . . .
Shall we live as slaves or free men?
That's the question—choose your "Amen"!

Chapter 24

March 15, 1963: The Dobosi Painting Company

For Laszlo Dobosi, March 15 was the day when he became a free man! The Dobosi Painting Company quickly progressed. The Chevrolet auto was too small.

My husband came home from work. "Bring the children. I want to show you something."

We got down to the parking lot. He showed me a gray hearse! I looked at him and said, "But that is a hearse!"

But, he said, "Look how big it is! Everything will fit in it."

"Well. It is fine by me, if it is okay for your customers."

After awhile, one of Laszlo's customers said to him, "Please call before you get here. All our neighbors and we are scared to death that the hearse is coming."

My husband told him, "Then, I am going to paint it red." They agreed that would be very good.

The next day, he came home earlier from work and painted the gray hearse a bright red. Oh, my son was very happy. "Daddy, it looks like a fire truck! Very pretty," he said.

Laszlo had more work than he could handle. His advertisement was from word of mouth. I suggested he should hire some help. Two weeks passed and he complained, "Some people show up for work drunk. I have to send them home. Some people don't even show up and I counted on them. I hear behind my back, 'We are working for that refugee.'"

I asked my husband, "Did you send them away? A person like that can not be trusted."

109

The next day my husband said, "I am going to call Cseke Laszlo and ask him if he would be interested to come and be my partner."

"If you know him," I said. "When we were kids, we played together. I will leave it up to you."

He made a call. Cseke was very happy for the offer. He asked if we could rent an apartment for them, and they could move in two weeks. Cseke was not a painter, but my husband said he was going to teach him. The Cseke family came: wife Eva, and a three-year-old little girl.

In 1964, Laszlo took him in as a full partner. Also, his name was on the check book. That way, if he went to the paint store, he would be able to purchase what was needed. Not much time passed, and Cseke started bad-mouthing Laszlo. He would go and not come back for hours.

I told that to my husband. He said, "I explained to him that when a customer calls, I have to go give them an estimate for the job. Since the distance is far, it takes time."

Cseke showed he was not satisfied. My husband told him, "We are not tied together. You didn't bring anything into the company. And if you are not happy, you can go. I would not have any hard feelings and you are not worth much. And your wife, she is asking too much money for that and that. Last week was for a sewing machine. My wife doesn't have a sewing machine." Laszlo said, "My friend, think it over. It is not right that you are not trusting me. And don't sit over here and gossip to my wife. You are upsetting her."

Cseke said, "I am sorry."

At the end of October, Laszlo stopped at the bank to deposit a check. The bank manager saw Laszlo and told him to come in his office. He said, "Your partner was here and he wrote out all of your money."

My husband said, "I am going to knock his head off."

Mr. Johnson, the bank manager, said, "He is not worth it. You put his name on your check book. Within the law, you can not do anything. If you need money, the bank will loan it to you."

Laszlo said, "Here is a five hundred dollar check. It should be okay for a while."

My poor husband came home. He told me the story. And we were worried, since winter was coming, and the painters make their money in the summer time. Laszlo's customers found out and, since it was almost winter, they got a lot of inside work for Laszlo for the whole winter.

The Cseke family disappeared and we never saw them again. There was a big lesson to be learned here. A partnership could be a dangerous thing and you have to be very careful of it.

On November 11, 1963, everybody was crying. Our president, John F. Kennedy, got assassinated. The whole country was in mourning.

In the springtime of 1964, my husband said he was very grateful to me, since I had been saving up the money nicely. We should have a parking lot for a truck.

In April 1964, my husband came home with news. "I bought a house. The address is Braddock Road, Alexandria."

"And how much did the house cost?"

"Almost twenty thousand dollars."

We went with him to see the house. It was a quite neglected house. The children and I didn't like it. But, it was bought. We had loved living in the apartment. Everybody there was our friend. We never were lonely. It had a swimming pool for the children. It was just a nice place for us.

We moved in May 1964. We had a big yard, lots of trees and bushes, but no children anywhere to play with. I missed my neighbors very much. While the children were playing outside in the yard, we mothers discussed who needed a baby sitter, who needed what. We helped each other out. For example, when the muumuu dress came in style, while others were watching the children, I sewed muumuu dresses for everyone and we had fun.

Our house was ugly, with brown panels everywhere.

My husband went to work. We missed him very much. We couldn't wait for him to come home. We had no one all day to talk to. When he got home, we hung on him every minute. We even cried to him. He encouraged us to not worry. We would get to know the new neighbors.

We said, "But the house is ugly, too!"

But he kept on encouraging us. "It will be pretty, too! I will paint it." My husband worked on the house every weekend. I helped as much as I could. To cover up the ugly panels, it needed three or four coats of paint. He diligently worked on the house, since he was the one who had bought it.

We had lived there for three months, when the neighbor came over with her younger son. She said, "My name is Lila. The little boy's name is Bobby, and I have two more at home. Bobby is the younger one. He is eight years old." It seemed like little Laszlo was going to have a playmate. Lila seemed nice, too.

On the right side of our house, it looked like there is a little girl there, about the same age as Victoria, and her name was Lisa. I hoped they would be good friends.

We lived right across from the elementary school. Laszlo would be going to school in two years.

By September, my husband was coming along nicely with the house renovation. One more month and the carpet people would come to put a new carpet down. My husband painted me a beautiful, pale lilac bedroom.

We also met the Meszaros, people at the Washington Hungarian Club. They lived nearby here. Horvath Laszlo had brought out his wife and two children since they were left behind in Hungary in 1956. We saw each other often.

We were going into Washington for Hungarian Mass. We had nice conversations with the other Hungarians.

When October came, all of the Hungarian refuges remembered the 1956 Revolution, which happened nine years ago. It changed many people's lives.

Soon it would be Christmas. The house was prettier and prettier. We planned out where we were going to put the Christmas tree. We were very good friends with Lila and Jimmy. The children were very happy with their Christmas presents.

For New Year's Eve, Lila and Jimmy, the Horvaths, and the Meszaros; they were all coming, and we were going to celebrate New Year's Eve in our beautiful house.

One day in January 1965, the snow had been falling all morning. It was afternoon, and I was trying to keep the very long driveway snow-free so my husband would be able to drive up to the house. The children were busy building a snow man and woman, and having a lot of fun.

In March, at the end of the yard was a long fence of forsythia blooming. They were my little boy's favorite flowers. Everything was coming out of the ground: tulips, hyacinths, jonquils. The dogwood trees were blooming, the cherry trees were blossoming, and the grass was beautifully green everywhere. It looked like everyone got a new, green carpet. Everywhere my eyes looked, I saw the new and freshness. All I could say was, "Spring is beautiful!"

Chapter 25

March 1965: I Became an American Citizen

We heard the news that the Hungarian government was giving amnesty to some of the Hungarian refugees who had left the country. Right away, I decided to apply for American citizenship. We sent the necessary documents to the Immigration and Naturalization Service. I started to learn the American laws and history. I told my husband that he should become an American citizen, too. But, he didn't feel the need for it.

I began learning how to drive a car. In two weeks, I would get my driving license. I received a letter from the Immigration and Naturalization Service that I should come in to take a test. I was quite nervous, since I didn't know what they were going to ask of me.

There was a very pleasant gentleman who did the questioning. He even complimented me on how much I knew. He said they would inform me when I should come for the ceremony. I was very happy. Laszlo was still working on the house.

I received my driving license. We had a big, white Lincoln Continental. It seemed to me it covered the whole road.

I got a phone call from Julia. She asked if I had received my driver's license. I told her, "Just yesterday." Then she asked me to take her to the Arlington Hospital because her husband was there. I thought, *Wow! So far?* Then I told her, "I don't know the way."

She said, "I know the way."

I felt sorry for her. I didn't have the heart to say that I would not take her. Instead, I told her, "We are coming to pick you up."

We dropped her off at the hospital and started to return home. I thought, *I hope we can find our way home.*

Laszlo and Victoria sat quietly in the back seat. I thought, *Oh, gee, I wonder where we are.*

As soon as I was finished with my thought, my son said, "We are lost, aren't we? Call Daddy!" he yelled. I have to tell you, at that time we had no mobile telephone.

I reassured him, "We are not lost."

He yelled again "Yes we are! Yes we are!"

As I drove along, I saw the top of the little church. I was so happy. I said to the kids, "Do you see the top of the little church? We pass by that little church to go grocery shopping. Do you remember?"

My son said, "Oh, Yes!"

We were very happy to make it back home. I have to tell you that when their father drove, the two of them argue in the back seat. And when I drove, they are very quiet. One day, their father said, "How quiet the children are when you are driving."

I told him, "Yes they are."

And he said, "Why?"

I answered, "Because they are scared."

At the end of summer 1965, we go to the citizenship swearing in ceremony. I became a United States citizen. It was a very big day. I told my husband, "I am going home with the kids."

He asked, "When?"

I said, "For next year's Easter."

He said, "But I can't go yet."

I said, "I understand."

We sent our application for our American passports. The anticipation in me was tremendous. I hardly could wait until spring. It had been almost ten years. I wondered how Mother would look. My little sisters were grown. The six-year-old twins were sixteen years old, already. If I could, I would leave tomorrow. But, soon the winter would be here. We had to wait until spring time because of the weather. I would write to Mother. She would be very happy. "Dear Mother, I will be home with my two little children for Easter."

I went shopping. I wanted to take a present to everyone. The postman brought the passport. We went to the Hungarian Embassy for the visa. The only thing left was to get the plane ticket. In Falls Church, there was a TWA Travel Agency; we went there. Two children and a grown up. The children's tickets were half price. The total price was $1,200.10. That was a lot of money then. Now we had everything. The time would pass, too. I got a letter from Mother. She was unbelievably happy.

Trudi and Mooney came over. They told us Mooney had to go to Korea again. Too bad he had to leave before the holidays. The family was very unhappy when they were separated, especially during the holidays. But, Trudi knew she could come and visit us with her little girl, Linda, anytime. I knew time was going to go slower than a big old turtle, in spite of the fact that I had a lot of work. I took care of that big yard. Winter would be here soon. The holidays were coming. If I kept very, very busy, spring would be here in no time.

Back home, Mother arranged how many cars they needed to come and pick us up. She wrote in her letter that everybody would be at the airport. They were waiting for the day of our arrival. My mother-in-law was also waiting for us, eager to see her grand children and she was very sorry her son could not come yet.

The Christmas holidays were gone. At the end of the yard, the forsythia bushes had buds. That was a sign of spring. They had never been prettier. The very much anticipated spring was here!

Since we were going for three months, I wanted to leave with everything taken care of. My husband did not have much knowledge of the house work. The children were excited, too. I told them stories of the family. We had a big, big problem. The children didn't speak Hungarian. Because of that, I was going to be very embarrassed at home. Everything happened so quickly that I didn't have time to teach them Hungarian. All our suit cases were packed. We were leaving the next day. I thought, *I probably won't be able to sleep all night.*

Chapter 26

April 10, 1966: I Am Going Home

On April 10, the long-awaited day had come. At 5:00 PM, the plane would leave with us. On April 11, 1966 at 1:00 PM, we would land in Budapest, with God's help.

The children enjoyed themselves on the plane. They took turns sleeping in my lap. I woke them up when the plane was getting ready to land. It had been such a long time since I had seen my little country. I can't describe my feeling when the plane wheels touched the ground. Is it true? I am here? After so much sadness and tears?

We went through the customs, and got outside. I was looking. I wanted to find Mother. There was a group. I saw my mother. I yelled, "I am here, Mother!" I can not write down the feeling I had. It seemed like I had left a hundred years ago. There was Mother and Father, my brother, and eight young ladies, whose names I did not know!

Right after they introduced themselves to me, Mother and my brother decided who was going in which car. Then we were on our way to Szarazd, where Mother lives. It was a small town.

For days, I just looked at my sisters. I didn't know what to talk about. They were the same way. Once again, I felt like a stranger. Ten years is a very long time. I am sure everyone has been in a situation where they could hardly wait to get there and once you were there, didn't know what to do.

I was in the same situation. For Laszlo and Victoria, it was a great experience. The chickens in the yard. The well in the yard. The outhouse. Laszlo was five and a half years old. Victoria was four and a half. For their age, they did fine. But the language was very much missed.

Mother's cooking was the best. Next week for Easter, twelve grown ups and six children were coming. Mother had them sleeping all over in the neighborhood. Ham, kolbasz, hard boiled eggs, red painted eggs for the children, delicious pastry only Mother could bake—everything was ready. Everybody would be here with the noon train. The little Szarazd house was completely filled up with grown ups and children. We all enjoyed ourselves at Mother's place.

My brothers-in-law and my sisters didn't know what to ask of me besides what I could buy in the stores in America. I told them, "Everything that you can imagine and much more."

It appeared my sisters were financially better off than before, in 1956. It seemed like 1956 hadn't been completely in vain. My husband would be happy for that. We had a bigger house in America, but their children had a grandma, grandpa, aunts, uncles, and cousins. In that way, my children were poorer than they were. My children were missing all these people from their lives. I would have not chosen that way. Destiny did that without our agreement.

The holidays were over, and everyone went home on the one o'clock train to Dunaujvaros. The town's name was no longer Sztalinvaros. That was big progress! My brother-in-law had taken lots of pictures. Who knew when that beautiful big family would be under one roof again? I would spend one more week in Szarazd with the children, then we were going to Baja to my mother-in-law.

One of the neighbors had puppies. They were so round. They were so beautiful. The children held them practically all day. Mother's little chicks and baby ducks were such a sensation for the kids. Mother taught little Laszlo how to take the eggs from under the hens. It was very pretty there. It was quiet. Every tree was blooming. Across from the kitchen door was the flower garden. The flowers were racing to see which one would come out of the ground first. When we come back from Baja, I was sure the flower garden would be filled up with all kinds of flowers. Mother baked pastries for us to take on the train. In the afternoon, we would leave for Baja.

Mother said, "I will wait for you to come back."

The children were on a train for the first time. It was a very big experience for them. They counted the telephone poles, just like Anna and I did more than thirty years ago. We were crossing a bridge over the Danube

River, and Laszlo and Victoria asked why the train slowed down so much. I said to them, "So you can see the fish in the Danube River." Well, they didn't take their eyes off the Danube's water.

Pretty soon, we stopped at the train station in Baja, my husband's home town. My sisters-in-law, Aranka and Gitta, were waiting for us. I was very happy to see my mother-in-law, whom I loved. The house and the yard were swept up and it looked like they were waiting for company.

In the yard was a tremendous, big mulberry tree. The branches hung down far enough that Laszlo was able to reach the berries. He stood under the tree and ate them many times during the day.

Mamma said, "Pretty soon the rest of the relatives will be here." The house was filled up with people very shortly. Sarika was a grown up now who, just eleven years ago was so unhappy to have to share her beloved uncle with another woman. Of course, everybody was sad because their brother was not able to come home. They pretty fast decided which child looked like them. They asked me how long we were going to stay. I told them two weeks. One of the sisters said how much they valued that they were able to see their brother's children.

After a week, Mother came. I was very happy to see her. She was worried we were not going to come back to Szarazd because I had had a little misunderstanding with Father over the children. I reassured her not to worry, that we would come back. But, first, we were going to Dunaujvaros. Mother was going back to Szarazd and, in a week, she would come to Dunaujvaros too. There we would be together again.

In Baja, we had a couple of more days. There was not much to do there. I was waiting to go to Dunaujvaros. I wondered if the people would recognize me. I wanted to know my sisters again. I wanted to see them. I wondered how Dunaujvaros had changed, besides the name; the town where I was so happy with my husband during our newlywed time. It seemed that, for a year, we had no cares, only to love each other with passionate sexual desire. But that all changed on that terrible October day. Ten years had passed since that lovely time. Homesickness and loneliness stepped in their place. The immigrant's bread is bitter. The beautiful red apple is tasteless!

We lived day by day, with the hope that we would, one day again, live in our own country, where the Akacfa flowers bloom. The sweet fragrance covers the area. That is the hope from day by day, from year to year. Hopefully, one day it will come. Oh, but hope not too many years will pass.

I told the children, "Tomorrow, we are going to Dunaujvaros."

They said, "But, make sure we are going on the train." They liked it so very much. They were not bored for a minute.

We arrived in Dunaujvaros on a beautiful spring afternoon. The spring fragrance hung in the air. The sun was very bright but also very pleasant. I looked at the buildings. The movie theater, the Gold Star Hotel, the post office; everything was there. I realized it was just the way I had left it. We walked on the sidewalk, further. Someone grabbed me, and spun me around. When my feet touched the ground again, I was able to see she was one of my co-workers. She said excitedly, "You are here!" Oh, we were so happy to see each other.

My dearest twin sister was also waiting. It was good to be together again, since I missed her so very much.

Dunaujvaros was a small city with five- and ten-story apartments and pretty parks. The fountains have frogs with water coming out of their mouths. Not just the children, but the grown ups like them, too. I shouldn't forget; there is an ice cream cart on every corner. Zsa Zsa and John, Anna's children, were good playmates for Laszlo and Victoria.

Mother arrived in Dunaujvaros. She was very happy to come since all of her children, besides the twins, lived here. They were still in school. Shortly, they would be finished with their accountant's education. Then, they, too, would work in Dunaujvaros.

Mother's plan was working out. None of her children would be stranded in Szarazd. Anna was working in the art gallery in the buffet. In the morning, we went there, so we would be together. In the corner was a small table. Mother and my other sisters were sitting around it.

Two young men came in the door. They went right up to the counter to Anna. One of them said to her, "When is Elizabeth going to come home?"

Anna pointed into the corner. She said to him, "She is right there!"

He looked and came right up to me. Then he said, "My beautiful love, how did I miss you?"

I was startled! I was nervous.

"Have you forgotten me?"

I had not forgotten him. He was the one who cursed me, and said to me, "You will cry where no one will see you." He was the one who wished that on me. Yes, I had cried. I had cried a lot, and no one saw me through the many years, just because I didn't love him back. I would put him in the past.

We really enjoyed ourselves. I was sorry my husband was not with us. He wrote a lot of letters and told us how much he missed us. It had been two months since we left our American home. We had one more month before we had to return. We strolled on the beautiful Danube concourse.

My brother offered to watch the children tomorrow so I could really enjoy the day. But, we had forgotten the language problem. The end of the day, my brother told me how the day had gone. He said, "I bought her ice cream. I bought her soda. But she was telling me something. So I bought her another ice cream, another soda, but she was still telling me something. I thought, 'My God. I hope she doesn't want anymore ice cream or soda'. A man came on the sidewalk and started to talk to Victoria. Then he turns to me. He said, 'Sir, would you please take the little girl to the bathroom?' I asked the man, 'Is that what she wants?' 'Yes, sir.'"

The day ended pleasantly for the three of them.

We went back to Szarazd with Mother, to spend a week there. The flower garden was absolutely beautiful. From my husband, I had a few letters to read. He couldn't complain hard enough as to how he missed us. I asked Mother, "How many young people are living here in Szarazd."

She said, "Just a few. The rest of them all left."

Geza, he lives here. He was my very first boy friend. I should write to Laszlo right away that we will be home soon.

I noticed Mother was lonely in Szarazd without her children. It was so different when all of us were home. Now it was quiet. She was not used to that. Mother didn't know what to do with herself. Often she traveled to Dunaujvaros. Father was working at the railroad. When he got home in the evening, after supper, he liked to go down to the restaurant. He used to say that was where he took care of business.

Our time was up. We have to leave. Mother was not so worried since she had been able to see me. Everybody was going to come with us to the airport. Now I knew my sisters' names. Now I was leaving grown ups behind. Ten years ago, they were just little girls. I hoped from now on I would see them much more often.

Laszlo was waiting for us at the Dulles Airport with excitement. In the house, there were ribbons everywhere. "Welcome home! Welcome home!" He urged me to tell him everything, everything.

I began. "The bureaucracy is big. You have to register in the police station. You have to let them know at the police station that you are leaving. One day, I hope that will not be necessary. I think we are going to need a little time to get back into the American way of living. One thing is very sure; I am going to miss everyone terribly."

Since we had a big back yard of three quarters of an acre, my husband said he was going to build a swimming pool. Right away, he started shoveling the hole where the swimming pool was going to go. He spent all his free time in the hole. He shoveled it and he shoveled it. Finally, after six months, he had a tremendous big hole. Then, the concrete truck came. It blew the concrete on the side and bottom of the hole. After that, Laszlo brought home bags and bags of white cement and lots and lots of slate for the patio part. He said he needed all of that for the swimming pool. Did I already tell you? He spent all of his free time in the hole.

By the end of May, and ten thousand dollars later, the swimming pool was completed. It looked like a home-made dress. The neighbor kids and ours just loved it. I didn't know what kind of project my husband would start after that. He needed to cover up his homesickness. While I was pregnant with my son, he was building a sixteen-foot boat in some big garage. We used it once. Then we bought a sixteen-foot aluminum boat.

He worked. I took care of the children. I cut the grass in that big, big, yard. I kept the swimming pool clean. I cooked every day. That is how the days and weeks passed.

When I told him one Sunday, "Let's us go somewhere," he resentfully told me I wouldn't let him rest.

The Horvath family, the Meszaros family, Lila with the boys, Trudi with Linda; they came often. The kids loved the pool. But, I would have liked to go somewhere, sometime, too. At a time like that, I missed my mother, my sisters, and the city the most.

In 1967, the Viet Nam War was going on. We watched them on the TV, night after night. I don't know what would have happened if we watched something else. But, he wanted to see what was happening. And whoever is more forceful, usually they are the ones who win.

Trudi and Mooney came back from Germany. They stayed with us for a few days. I cooked dinner, and they were down in the TV room watching the news, at six that night. They yelled, "Come down! Come down!"

On April 4, 1968, Martin Luther King was assassinated. I knew right away that was terrible news. The colored people started rioting. They were breaking into stores, setting fires; acting like they had lost their minds. The white people were in danger. We were extremely saddened by Dr. King's assassination. It was a tremendous loss to the country, to lose such a brilliant person.

"Let's move home." I don't even know how it started, but I told my husband. "You have to go home, find out if you will be able to get a job, find out if you will be able to support us. If that all is possible, then you buy us a house. Towards the football stadium, I saw some nice little houses."

Chapter 27

May 18, 1968: Laszlo Goes to Hungary

On May 18, 1968, he got himself a passport and was on his way to Hungary. In Budapest, he rented a car. In Dunaujvaros, he bought us a one-bedroom apartment. They had just started building them; therefore, he didn't even see what he bought. My brother jealously told me he hardly spent any time in Dunaujvaros. It looked like he had spent most of his time in Baja, not where he was planning to live with his family. When he came home, a month later, he said the apartment would be ready in September. After that, we could move.

Chapter 28

October 1968: We Moved Back to Hungary

In October 1968, we sold the house, got a small container, and filled it up. We also took one 1966 Oldsmobile Cutlass automobile. They shipped the car to Bremerhaven. We said goodbye to all of our friends. They were sorry we were leaving.

We arrived in Bremerhaven on a Saturday, in the early afternoon. Of course, everything was closed. We had a day and a half in Bremerhaven. It was October 20, and the weather was foggy and cold. In the port, there was a very old ship, a few hundred years old. We looked at it, then wondered what else should we do.

We went to dinner. Since the menu was completely unknown to us, we asked the waiter to recommend something for dinner. Well, how should I say it? That was a very big mistake. After dinner, we were all still hungry. We said to ourselves that the breakfast would probably be better. Nobody can ruin eggs. Right? Wrong! We couldn't wait for it to be Monday so we could get our car and be on our way.

On Monday, early in the morning, my husband left for the port to pick up the car. We were thinking that in a short time, he would be right back, and we would be able to be on our way. By two in the afternoon, I was really worried. We wondered where he could be. Maybe something happened to him? Maybe something hit him? Where would I go look for him?

For hours, we sat on the edge of the bed in that hotel room. The hotel room can be very boring. I thought, *I will wait a little longer, then I should start out to look for him. Oh, no, because maybe he will come in the meantime, then they will have to come looking for me. I can't leave the children by them-*

selves, either. I told myself, *He will be here, any second.* The children were very quiet. Worry set in on their little faces.

A couple of minutes before four in the afternoon, there was a knock on the hotel room door. All three of us ran towards the door. I can't even write down how relieved we were. It didn't matter what had happened. The main thing was, Daddy was back.

My husband said, "Let's go! Let's go! I will tell you in the car."

"It is almost dark."

"That's all right, let's get out of here."

What happened was that the car got scratched on the boat. They said the damage was $180, and my husband should pay it! That was completely crazy! We were the victims. Why should we pay for it? We even had purchased insurance. The German at the pier said, "When you get to Hungary, the company is going to send the $180 to you." The reason was so we would not sue them for the damage, and they wouldn't give him the car until he gave them a hundred and eighty dollar check. Since that time, fifty years have passed, but it still doesn't make any since.

The main thing was that we were on our way! It was dark and raining very hard. The Germans were just flying on the Autobahn. Then the traffic slowed down. A man with a yellow rain coat and a lamp in his hand was detouring the traffic to the side road. Because of that, everybody had to slow down, pretty much.

Soon after we got on the side road, we felt like somebody ran into our car. As soon as we got ourselves together, my husband got out of the car, but no one was behind us. It was obvious something had happened to the engine. My husband pushed the car off of he road by himself. No one stopped to help. He opened the hood and, with the help of the flashlight, he saw the carburetor screw was missing. With a lot of luck, in the tool box, he found a screw. He was able to fix the car. We were very luck the traffic had been detoured off the very fast Autobahn. If that had happened on that fast Autobahn, surely we would have been run over. And that would not have been a pretty sight.

Before we left America, Lila bought each of us a necklace with St. Christopher, who watches out for the travelers. And he did watch out for us!

We decided we would stop in the next town. Luckily, it wasn't too far. At ten o'clock at night, we were in a nice hotel. Dinner would be good since we hadn't eaten since morning. My husband decided that, in the morning, he would have the car checked out in the garage.

We were heading towards Munich. We decided to buy a nice station wagon in Munich. We were going to sell the Oldsmobile since, at that time, if somebody wanted to buy a car in Hungary, they had to wait two or three years.

We made nice time. I read a map and Laszlo drove. Near Munich, I said, "Slow down; you are outdoing the Germans!"

He said, "You can get the hang of it!"

The children were fine and seldom argued. We had made them a comfortable place in the back seat. They were even able to sleep. We told them they did not need to ask every half hour, "When are we going to get there?" When we got there, we would let them know.

Once in Munich, we went to the auto dealer. We bought a Volkswagen. They had to order it. When it was done, they would send it to us in Hungary.

We stopped for lunch. It was too bad, but we left my son's nice winter coat in the restaurant. When we realized it, we were too far to go back. We thought it would not be a problem to buy him another one, but it was. With God's help, we would be in Vienna the following Thursday evening.

I read the map. We hadn't got lost yet. Our route was long. We had time to think. I wondered how our life would be at home. Surely, it was going to be a big change. Well, it didn't matter; we were on our way.

There was a quiet rain falling. It was about 6:00 PM, and the city of Vienna was sparkling everywhere from the evening light. It was very pretty. Our feelings told us we were in Europe. My husband asked, "Will that hotel be okay?"

"Yes."

We took a hotel room, then had dinner. We knew the children liked Weiner schnitzel. I asked the waiter, "Do you have Weiner schnitzel?"

He said, "But, madam, you are in Vienna!"

Of course, we ordered the dinner of Weiner schnitzel. After the dinner, my husband said, "That was a lot of sitting. I am going to take a walk and stretch my legs."

I put the children in bed. I thought, *I am going to wait for my husband.* But I was tired too, so I fell asleep. I woke up at 2:00 AM and I saw my husband's bed was empty. *Oh, my God! Where is that man?* Of course, I thought the worst. *Something hit him! Somebody knocked him down! Somewhere, he is lying injured or dead! And, I am here with two little children.* Then, I got mad. *Just wait! Why is that man creating so much worry for me?*

At 3:00 AM, there was a knock on the door. When I opened the door; he was standing in front of me, half intoxicated. He told me what good company he had had. He said, "I went into that restaurant. There was a table where Hungarians were sitting. I introduced myself to them. Then we were singing. I haven't felt myself that wonderful for many years!"

Just like an understanding wife, I forgave him. He had scared the living daylights out of me. So, I told him, "You have to sleep fast. Morning will be here shortly and we have a very big day ahead of us. We have to be home by afternoon."

After breakfast, at 11:00 AM, We went to look for some car parts my brother needed. He asked us to bring them to him from Vienna. Finally, we located the parts he asked for.

We were finally on our way home! We were sort of nervous. We got to the Hegyeshalom border. There were soldiers with weapons hanging off of them. As we got out of the car, right away, they got hold of it. They practically tore it apart. When they realized I didn't like what they were doing, one told me I should go into the building with the children. I did just that.

In a long while, two soldiers came in the door, with my husband between them. They went straight up the stairway. They motioned for me to stay. Our passports were in their hands. My children and I had American passports. My husband had a white passport, for a man without a country.

Finally, after a few hours, we were on our way. My husband was very quiet. I asked him what happened upstairs. He didn't want to tell me. I said, "You must tell me what happened up there in the office!"

He reluctantly started to talk. "They said, 'Hungary is not a revolving door.' They said I should watch my mouth, or I could get myself into a lot of problems. 'Not allowed to do propaganda,' they said. 'Maybe you came to do propaganda for America.'"

That all played down with a lot of aggression. That brought back a fear into my husband and into me, too. I angrily said to him, "Why didn't you tell me this back at the border?"

My husband said, "Then what would you have done?

"Right away, we would have turned back to Vienna."

He said, "I didn't think about that! Now it is too late."

We reached Gyor. We noticed we had a flat tire. We stopped along the side of the road and started to change the tire. In a few minutes, we were surrounded with people. Everybody wanted to know what was the horsepower in that car. How fast did it go? At that time, probably that was the only Oldsmobile in Hungary.

The welcome home at the border didn't leave our thoughts. How nice it would have been for them to have said, "Welcome to Hungary!" That way it would have been so beautiful. We would have been flying with happiness. But now, we were broken down. We were told to shut our mouths. We were scolded. How were we going to cover that up in front of Mother and the others? They would see it on us. And, we were not even allowed to tell them. We felt like when an animal is caught in a cage.

We arrived in Dunaujvaros, our new home. We had dreamed of that day for the past twelve years. That was what we were wishing for: to be in our country, with our fellow Hungarians, and to hear our Hungarian language.

The relatives were all present. Mother was very happy since all of her children were at home.

In the morning, we went to see the apartment my husband had purchased. We walked in mud up to our ankles. The sidewalk was not finished yet. We stepped into the apartment. We saw four doors, right away. There was a very tiny, narrow kitchen. Right next to it was a toilet. On the side was the bathroom. From the bathroom was another door, into a long, small, narrow bedroom. From the hallway, you stepped into the living room. I counted eight doors.

Also, there was a big, long balcony which was absolutely not useable. The city bus stopped right there. And when a bus starts up, the black smoke just oozes out of the end of the bus. In the meantime, I looked at the place and wondered how I could make a home out of an apartment that had so many doors.

I looked at my husband. "Tell me, where was your brain when you bought this thing for us?"

His answer was, "There was no other one."

But, of course, we had been talking about a house, not a tiny apartment filled up with doors.

Well, we had to go buy furniture so we would have a place to sleep.

Four days after we got home, that night, there was a knock on the door. Two civilian men were standing at the door. They invited themselves in. They asked my husband when he was planning to go to work. As you know, everybody has to work here. No one can just hang around. We said, "First, we have to set up our household."

My husband said, "In two weeks, I will look for a job."

When they left, they said, "You should see to it that you have a job very soon."

I hope we overcome that, too.

Chapter 29

Police and "American Propaganda"

We signed the kids into school. The container came too, with our stuff. My husband was on his way to find a job.

From the window, I could see him coming. He said, "Tomorrow, I am going to work."

"But where?"

"Painting the stairways."

Well, it was not the White House, but stairs needed to be painted, too. My husband was a very good tradesman. He learned some things in America. When he tried to show the company what was easier and better, the manager was not interested.

My husband was in the gas station, buying gas. Somebody asked him, "How much does that huge thing eat? And how much does it cost in America to fill it up?"

My husband said, "Five dollars."

The man said, "How long do you have to work for that?"

"One hour."

The next day, we received a post card from the police station. They want my husband to come in, to the third floor. We looked at each other, and wondered what they wanted. On the designated day, we were in the police station on the third floor. I had to stay outside in the hallway.

As I waited there, I remembered our border crossing into Hungary, when they took him upstairs and they roughly scolded him. As I was thinking, my palms started sweating. Finally, forty minutes later, he came out of the door. I could see he was very emotionally stirred up.

They were asking, "So, why are you propagandizing for America? That is why you came here?"

My husband told them, "I came home with the proper documents."

"Why are you lying?" they said. "You can fill up your big car with an hour's wages?"

He said, "That is not a lie!"

They said, "Don't say it."

"But they asked me."

"It doesn't matter; don't say it."

"Then what should I say?"

"Nothing! Don't say anything or you will be in big trouble!"

He remembered at the gas station a dentist was asking all of those questions. We were amazed! Why did a man like that need to be an informer? We were hoping that was the end of that. But it wasn't. They called him into the police station often. They accused him of saying one thing and another thing. "You talk too much," they said. Of course, the people were asking questions; not necessarily political things, but just questions about the everyday lifestyle in America.

It was very hard to tolerate our life in our country. We cried often. It looked like, as soon as they could find something so they could have some sort of a reason, they would arrest him.

The year of 1956 had not been forgotten. They knew he was one of the leaders. Our lives were full of fear. Our money was going fast. We decided this was a dangerous place for my husband and we had to go back to America. You can't live in fear.

We had to make sure they did not send the station wagon we had bought in Munich. Besides, we would have to pay 100 percent customs for it! On the telephone, I called the man who we purchased the car from. Of course, I couldn't tell him, "Don't send the car because we are not going to stay here." I told the man we couldn't receive the car because of unforeseen circumstances. "I am sorry, but I can't explain further," I said to him.

He said, "Don't worry. I understand. Where would you want me to send the money?"

I did feel he really understood our situation. I told him to send it to America and I gave them Lila's address. He reassured me not to worry. That was where he would send the price of the car. Even today, I think of that man with love. And, that happened forty years ago!

We received a letter from Lila. They had received the money from Munich and she put it in the bank. We decided we would like to leave Hungary legally. We filled out the documents and we turned them in to the government. We received the answer. "At this time we are not able to grant your wish."

One of our acquaintances said he knew a person in Budapest in the government. He would talk to him. Maybe he could help. A couple of days later, the man said he had good news! His friend would be able to help, but he needed six hundred dollars. We were happy. We had hope. We gave him the six hundred dollars. After many months, we had to realize he was nothing but a crook!

My husband and I put our heads together again. We came to the conclusion that he would go and live in Baja. Since the county seat for Baja was in Kecskemet and we were not known there, maybe he could get travel documents to go to Yugoslavia to go visit his relatives there. That was the hope.

In the meantime, he lived with one of his sisters. To pass the time, he taught young guys wrestling, since he had been a wrestling champion. I was in Dunaujvaros with the children. So we lived separately. The children missed their father tremendously. They were used to his being home every night.

My brother accused me of being separated. He was very upset. I tried to tell him we were not separated. "Then why is he not home?" he asked me.

I said, "Because he makes more money there." But, he didn't like the whole thing. I think he missed my husband, who was a very entertaining man. Nobody was bored around him.

For three months, my poor husband was not with us. He came home on each Sunday. When he was leaving Sunday night on the bus to get to the train station, my little boy walked him to the bus stop. My husband told me he would run beside the bus as far as he could and it almost broke his heart.

At the end of June, one Saturday evening, my husband came home. He said, "Today I received my travel documents for visiting Yugoslavia."

Sunday morning at six o'clock, the bus would be leaving and he would be on it. He had come to say goodbye. Of course, we did not say anything to the children. An hour later, he had to be going. The Oldsmobile wasn't sounding very good, and it could not break down and make him miss the bus. The relatives had used the car for moving and they had over-loaded it.

Chapter 30

June 28, 1970: Laszlo is Free Again

On Monday, June 28, 1970, at three in the afternoon, the postman came. He brought me a telegram from Austria, from my husband. We had a big map. Right away, I spread it out on the living room floor. I looked up the Austrian town where the telegraph was sent from.

Well, my husband had for the second time gained back his freedom. The first time was in 1956. I thanked God for helping him regain his freedom once more. He would have wound up in the prison sooner or later since he loved his country too much. He couldn't allow it when they were hurting it. I looked at our two little children. I felt we were orphaned. Then I thought, *Even if we are not going to meet again, if that is what destiny wants, I will accept it.* But my husband had to live as a free man.

I received the first letter. My poor husband wrote down in a letter that he was in Yugoslavia in a big, big forest. The family of wild boars chased him up on a tree. He had to hang on the tree for hours while it was raining like crazy. The tree was very slippery from all of that water oozing down. Hours later, the boars left. But one of his shoe's heels was in a boar's mouth. Finally, he was able to get down from the tree. He couldn't straighten his arm out because he got a cramp from holding the tree for so long. It was very early morning. The sun started to come up. He came out of the forest. He saw farming land which had a scare crow on it. He went closer and noticed the scare crow was stuffed with newspapers. They were not Hungarian newspapers. They were Austrian newspapers! He was very happy since he had had no idea where he was.

After a month of my husband being on free land, he couldn't stand it any longer. He needed to hear my voice. We had no telephone. He called my twin sister, hoping he would find us there.

At eight o'clock at night, there was a knock on the door. I wondered who had come; it was late. It was my twin sister with her daughter. She said, "I am concerned."

I asked, "What is the problem?"

She said, "I talked to Laszlo. He telephoned."

Right away, I acted like he had telephoned from Baja.

My twin sister said, "He is in Austria. But, you know that. And you didn't tell any of us!"

"Yes, I didn't tell you, so you won't get into trouble."

My twin sister started crying. "How big a big burden and sorrow you are carrying! And you have no one to tell."

That was the truth. Since my husband was in a safe place, I had started working on the departure of my children and me.

I was in Budapest at the American Embassy. I told the ambassador that my husband had left, and I needed the embassy's help. I thought that it would not be too hard, since we were American citizens, the three of us: the children and me.

The ambassador told me that they knew where my husband was and that they were in touch with the Austrian Embassy. But he was extremely sorry. He was not allowed to give me my passport until I brought the release documents from the Hungarian government. The Hungarian government said I had a dual citizenship. Since I was living in Hungary, I was, therefore, under the Hungarian government rules. But he reassured me my American passport was in the safe; they had got it back from the Hungarian government. The ambassador recommended that I hire a lawyer. They gave me three names.

I looked one of them up. When I told him why I had come, he said to me, "Madam, if you would be Mrs. Nixon, even then we could not help you." By the way, Mr. Nixon was the president at that time.

Now, for a minute, the hope rug was pulled out from under me. That day was long. I had to go home. My little boy was waiting for me. He knew where I was—taking care of our going to see Daddy. That was the only way he would let me go. My little girl was too young, and she gossiped, too. I needed a few days to gather my thoughts and my energy, too. I didn't know what to do. I was skinny and I felt bad. I felt that life's burdens were too much.

My money was getting short, too. I started selling what I could. I needed to go to see a doctor. But I felt it was not a physical problem I had. A year and a half of constant stress was too much. One of my sisters gave me a woman doctor's address. She said, "Go see her."

I went to the lady doctor hoping maybe she could help. She examined me. She knew it was not a physical problem that I had. She sat down, and she said, "Let's talk."

I felt comfortable with her. I told her where my husband was and what had happened since we had moved home. She told me, "Monday, I am going to the Budapest State Department." She wanted me to write a letter which stated what I had told her, and she would hand-deliver it. That was on a Friday. I thanked her very, very much. I knew that wonderful woman was going to help me.

I already felt some of the stress lifted off me. My guardian angel had a hand in that. That was the fifth miracle.

I said goodbye to the doctor. I told her, "Tomorrow, I will be back with the letter."

As soon as I got home, I put the paper on the table with a pen in my hand. I looked at the white paper. How should I write that? I had never written such an important letter in my entire life. I said to myself, "I will write down what has happened and what kind of situation I am in." Yes, we were guilty. We had dared to hope, after twelve years of exile, maybe, just maybe, we would be able to live in our beloved little country, and also with parents, siblings, cousins, friends; we were hoping that would be possible. But, human jealousy and bad wishes, they are mighty powerful.

The next day, with my finished letter, I ran to the bus station to get to the doctor's house. I was standing in the yard with my doctor who was just about to go grocery shopping. I handed my letter over to her. She started reading it. I had started my letter, "Dear Mr. Benko," My doctor said, "Oh no, I said write it to me!"

I apologized, "I am sorry, I misunderstood."

In the meantime, she read it. When she got to the end of my letter, she said to me, "We are not going to change anything—not a word! I am taking it just the way it is."

I thanked her and said goodbye. I reassured my ten year old little boy that I had done everything possible. Now we just had to wait.

In the meantime, my husband wrote a letter to our American neighbor, Lila. He told her we were planning to come back to America. Lila, right away, sent us plane tickets; one to my husband in Vienna, and the other three into Budapest to the travel agency. The travel agency in Budapest sent me a letter. They informed me they had received three plane tickets and I should come, with the necessary documents, and pick them up. Well, I boarded a bus and went to Budapest. In the travel agency, I told them I was sorry, but I didn't have the necessary documents like a passport. They were very nice. They told me they would hold on to my plane tickets until I come back. Then I said goodbye to them.

The days passed slowly. I had done everything. I had to wait. Life is unpredictable, but I was hoping. Sometimes it is just the hope that keeps a man alive.

My little boy got sick. He got strep throat. I took him to the doctor every day for a shot. One afternoon, Victoria was at her girl friend's house playing. I thought, *I am going to lie down for a short nap.* Ten minutes passed. Victoria's friend, Edit, ran into our apartment yelling, "Mrs. Dobosi, Victoria got hit with a motor bike."

I ran down to the street. My little girl was already standing, and she was arguing with someone. It looked like she was all right. I took her into the hospital to have her checked out. Nothing was broken. She had a slight concussion and bruises on her upper thigh. They kept her overnight for observation.

She was lucky, since the motor bike threw her onto the grass. What happened was the bus was standing still, and people were getting off. She wanted to cross the street. In the meantime, the motor bike came out from behind the bus and he hit Victoria. He was at fault. I managed to get over my fright.

The thought entered into my mind: how would I stand in front of their father with one child? The thought haunted me. I couldn't sleep. I tried to get my mind off it. I hardly let the children out of the apartment after that.

On day, there was a knock on the door. A strange woman stood there. She introduced herself. She started telling me her husband had an accident with a motor bike. He broke his leg and the motor bike was damaged, too. And that was going to cost money to get it fixed! They thought I should give them money!

I said to her, "Woman, whose idea was that nonsense, or are you playing a terrible joke on me?" She looked at me very surprised. I said to her, "Your husband almost killed my only little girl. It was your husband's fault. I still can't sleep. Now, you come here and ask me for money? Please explain to me what urged you to do such a thing. Your husband knew it was his fault he hit my little girl."

She showed the embarrassment she was having. She asked me for forgiveness and she left. I never saw them again.

What I think happened is that somebody must have told them, "Go to the Americans; they probably have a lot of money." That is the name they gave us in Dunaujvaros. That is how we were known. Not the Dobosi name. My husband told them we did have a name.

I told the kids we were going to see their grandmother in Szarazd. They were very happy.

Zsa Zsa, John, the cousins; they would be coming, too. Anna and Maria would be leaving with us. Mother and Father didn't know we were coming, but they were so happy when they saw us! The younger twins, Magdi and Victoria, were finished with their schooling. They were both certified accountants and they worked in Dunaujvaros. In that house, where ten children grew up, there were only two grown ups living there now.

I could see the fright on them. What would happen from now on? They were only sixty years old. There was no money for the golden age. No money for travel. To close the door after all the children are grown up it is a relief. But they were also seeing how lonely their days would be. I started really feeling sorry for them. I was almost crying. Mother said, "Elizabeth what are you thinking?" I was afraid to tell her my thoughts, but she urged me to tell her, "What is the problem."

"Okay, I will tell you. When we go back to America, you and Father should move to Dunaujvaros, into my apartment if you like."

She started to cry. "Oh, no, no! I would rather have you stay here."

I told her that was not possible. I was trying to convince her how nice it would be in the warm city apartment. The doctors were there, the hospital was close by, and most of all, all her children. "You won't have to worry about each other."

So we decided. They agreed to move to Dunaujvaros. In the meantime, I was completely convinced that we had to move home in that uncertain political time. When I think back, it seems like when a person is caught in a whirlpool and it just spins them; they go down. It felt like that was what happened to us.

It seems to me, now, that the reason why we had to move home was so Mother and Father would have a place near where their children were living. They deserved it. They had sacrificed a lot to raise up that many children in such difficult times. They deserved everything good, and more.

I was completely sure that, shortly, I would receive my passport. I think everything has a reason. Without us, Mother and Father would have had to live in Szarazd the rest of their lives.

Father's wish came true, too. One time, the two of us were sitting on the patio. He was telling me that he prayed to God that he would not be stuck in Szarazd. I was very surprised at what he said. At that time, I did not know that one day they would live in Dunaujvaros.

The children were really enjoying themselves. They chased the chickens when their grandmother could not see them. Then they would go up into the hay mow and jump down, even though that was not allowed, because it was pretty high up there.

The next day, we planned to go back to Dunaujvaros. I wondered if we had mail. My husband, in his letter, was complaining about how much he missed us. I was going to write to him. I was going to tell him again that I had done everything, and now we had to wait. All he needed to do was to be patient.

At the end of September, the children were going to school. I had lived for eight months separate from my husband. The days were dragging.

I had a very dear neighbor. Her name was Margit. We became good friends. I valued her friendship.

In the middle of October, the post man came. He handed me a post card. I read it. "Madam, You and your two children's departure is granted. Don't go anywhere. You will be notified further."

My happiness was extreme! I boarded a bus with my post card in my hand. I went to see my doctor and friend to let her know the news about what she had helped me to achieve. When she saw me, she said, "I am so glad you came."

I handed her my post card. She said, "I know! I know! I was informed, but I didn't know your address."

She was very happy, along with me. I thanked her very much. We said goodbye.

After ten days since I received my post card, I wondered how long I would have to wait to hear more. I decided to go into the police station. I asked the captain, "Please call to Szekesfehervar to see whether my passport is there." He said to me they don't like to call to the higher ups. I thought, *What a coward!*

I took a bus to Szekesfehervar. When I got there, the secretary was in the office. I told her, "I came for my passport. Did Budapest send it already?" She pointed to the medium-sized cabinet. It has glass doors. I saw my passport!

She said. "Yes, here it is," and pointed to my passport." She said, "The captain is not here right now, but he will be here shortly. In the meantime, you could go to the post office and buy the necessary documentary stamps."

I already felt like a bird—free! By the time I got back from the post office, the captain was in the office, too. Before he handed the passport over to me, he asked me if he could give me some advice.

I said, "Sure!"

He said, "The next time you are doing big things, would you think it over more carefully?"

I said to him, "The whole situation is very sad."

He said, "Yes, it is."

As I went to the bus station, many thoughts were in my mind. I had a lot to do. Shots. What could we take with us since we are emigrating out of the country? We needed a Visa from the Austrian Embassy. I had to go pick up the plane tickets. I also had to go to the American Embassy to pick up my American passport.

I had to hurry to the bus. It would leave in a few minutes for Dunaujvaros. When I got home, I had to find my brother. I needed his help. He had a car.

When my brother found out Laszlo was in Austria, and I was joining him with the children, my brother said, "Now here it is. You are coming and going. And we are here trying to wrack our brain on how to get out of here."

Of course, he did not know what it took to get here. We had to be careful what we told him, as he liked to drink, and then he talked too much. My little son would be very happy that we would be with Daddy pretty soon. We didn't tell anything to the little girl. It was better that way. Mother was coming at the end of the week. I could hardly wait. There was so much news to tell.

We were going to Budapest with my brother. One thing after the other, we were taking care of everything.

The first trip was to the American Embassy. I was congratulated by the ambassador. He said, "You have taken care of the impossible!" If you will remember, the lawyer said he could not help me, even if I were Mrs. Nixon. I had the plane tickets in my hand already. Next, we went to the Austrian Embassy. They were not too friendly. That was okay.

Next, we had to go to the Hungarian government. Oops, we missed them! They were only open until noon. We had to come back the next day. I was feeling very satisfied. We had taken care of a lot.

It looked like we could leave on October 26. Interesting! Two years ago, we had come through the Hungarian border on October 26. That was a very unpleasant memory.

My brother and I got home. The telegram was waiting for me from my husband. "I know you are coming and I am waiting for you!"

I thought that, since he knew we were coming, I didn't have to send him a telegram. Mother arrived. I told her, "You and Father may live here, in this apartment, as long as you are alive."

My brother and I went back to Budapest. I received permission for what I was allowed to take with us. It would fit into two suitcases. Only two days left. Father arrived. My sisters came. The time was short. I didn't think we would be missed very much. Twelve years is a long time. I felt my sisters were close in my heart. I was told back, on the other hand, that I was looked at as some distant aunt. I understood, but it still hurt. I thought, *Two suitcases, two children.*

I was hoping we still had some money at Lila's, from the price of the German car. Lila and the Horvath's were waiting for us. This was our last night in Hungary. The next afternoon, at two o'clock, the plane would leave for Vienna. My husband was waiting for us.

I started packing. I look at my wallet, and saw that it was pretty much worn out. I decide to change it for my spare, new wallet. As I transfer things into the new wallet, what did I see? I pulled it out. I couldn't believe my eyes! I looked at it. I looked at both sides. No matter how I looked at it, that was a hundred dollar bill! This was the sixth miracle.

I yelled out, "Hoo! Haa!"

Mother said, "What is the matter? What did you find?"

I showed it to her. Right away, a thought came into my mind, *We are going to need that tomorrow, desperately.*

Mother looked at me very sadly. I was very sad, too. I had to leave my beloved mother here again. I finished the packing. Both of the suitcases were filled up. Tomorrow, we would leave.

Chapter 31

October 26, 1970: We Three Are Leaving Hungary

On October 26, 1970, in the morning, I went to the school to pick up the children's report cards. The principal was very shocked when I told him why I had come. In a very short time, they brought out the children's report cards. I said goodbye and left.

At the Budapest Airport, the customs people very thoroughly checked our luggage. My husband had been collecting coins—like from the 1800s and unique coins—to give them to my son, since he was a coin collector. He had them in his pocket. I thought it would be better to put them in the suitcase.

While the customs officer was checking the suitcase, he came across the coin collection. He said, "What is that?"

I told him that was my son's coin collection.

He asked me, "Where is the permission?"

I told him, "I didn't think it was needed."

He said to me, "But these are American dollars!"

I told him, "No they are not. It is a child's collection of rare coins. That was only eight dollars."

"You have no permission and we are going to confiscate them."

"But that belongs to the child!"

"You are protesting not to give it up?"

In the meantime, from the window, I watched our plane being boarded. I asked him, "Is that plane over there ours?"

He said, "Yes!"

I told him we could not miss that plane. My husband was waiting for us.

"Then we will write a document and you are going to sign it without protesting. The money stays."

I told him again, "That is not money."

He told me, "As you wish; then you are not going!"

In the meantime, I was looking at our plane. The door was closing. Would that plane leave us behind? My husband's heart would break if we didn't get off that plane. It had already been four months that he had not seen us. I turned to my son and I said to him, "It is all right, your daddy is going to replace it."

Now, the ten-year-old boy began to cry. He was worrying, too, that we were going to miss the plane. I told the customs officers, "Go ahead. Prepare the document. I will sign it, if that country needs that eight dollar coin collection that much!"

He ran to a little office with me. They prepared the document, and I signed it. But he did give my son the three pennies.

They put us on something like a golf cart and drove us out to the plane. They opened the plane door and let the steps down. My children and I went up in the plane. Finally, we were sitting in our seats. I looked out the airplane window and I thought, *I hope my legs will break if I once more am going to put my feet on that cursed land.* This was the first time I didn't like my country.

I was very upset and knew I should calm down; very soon, we would land in Vienna and my husband would be there. The children relaxed in their seats.

My son said, "Look, Mother, we are landing!"

"Yes, I see it."

We were in the Vienna Airport. We looked right, we looked left; we did not see my husband anywhere. *My God! I wonder what is wrong with him, since he is not here. He must have been caught in the heavy traffic and he will be here any minute.* But, an hour and a half passed. Everybody else had gone. We were still in the middle of the room so he could see us.

I went up to the information desk. I asked them to please call the American Embassy for me. They did. There was a man on the telephone. I introduced myself to him, "I am Mrs. Dobosi and I am here at the airport with the children, but my husband was not here to pick us up."

He told me, "Sit tight, and we are going to find him." They knew he was supposed to pick us up. He told me to call them back in thirty minutes.

We waited for three hours. I asked the information counter to please call the embassy for me again. From the embassy, the man said, "We are looking for him, but we have not found him." He told me to call back in thirty minutes.

Thirty more minutes passed. At the counter, the people didn't want to make a phone call for me again. They showed me a telephone booth. Of course, I didn't have the proper money. I asked them at the counter, "Please, just one more time. Call the embassy for me."

The man from the American Embassy told me they had found him. He was on his way to the airport and he would be there shortly. I happily told my tired little children, "They found Daddy and he will be here soon."

At six o'clock at night, I thought, *Soon we will be swept out of here.* I heard the loudspeaker say, "Mrs. Dobosi, come up on the upper floor." I ran up and I saw no one. I happened to look back down there and my husband was already hugging and kissing the children.

So, I ran down. I asked him, "Why did you call me up there? Then you are not there! Are you stupid, or what?"

He told me, "While I was waiting for you, I looked down and I saw the children. Then I ran down." "

"All right, where have you been?"

He said, "At the train station!"

"What were you doing in the train station? You sent me a telegram telling me you were waiting for us. Why didn't you find out everything?"

He said, "Who thought you would take an airplane for that short distance?"

"But we had our plane tickets." Then I asked him, "Do you have any money?"

He said, "I have six dollars."

"Well then, the children are hungry, and where are we going to sleep?"

He said, "I thought you had some."

"From where? I sent you the six hundred dollar traveler's check you asked for. All right. Last night when I was packing, I found in my spare wallet a hundred dollar bill. I told Mother 'We are going to need that hundred dollars very much tomorrow.' Now, let's go. The children are hungry and we also need a hotel."

Finally! The family was together. My husband looked skinny and worn. I was going to cook again and he would be all right. He loved my cooking.

We had dinner in a nice little place. The children were at ease. They enjoyed the family being finally together again after such a long time. We found a hotel. We had money for the next day, too.

I asked my husband, "Do you have your plane ticket?"

He said, "It is at the TWA travel agency."

"Why is it there? Why didn't you pick it up?"

"Because my documents were not ready at the American Embassy."

"But how come it is not ready?"

He said, "It will be ready tomorrow."

"All right, but I am only able to stay in Austria until tomorrow."

He said, "It will be ready in the morning."

"Then after breakfast, we are going to the embassy to pick up your documents."

We put the children in bed. It had been a very hard day. We went to bed, too. It was wonderful lying in my husband's strong, loving arms again. We felt no one could hurt us. We fell asleep right away.

The next morning, we were awakened by the children's voices. It was time for breakfast.

Afterward, we went to the American Embassy. We were going to pick up Daddy's documents. The secretary said, "It is not ready."

I was very surprised. I said, "Why is it is not ready?"

The secretary asked me if I would like to speak with the ambassador.

"Yes, please," I answered her.

She took me into the ambassador's office. He held both of my hands. He said to me, "Mrs. Dobosi, let me congratulate you! We kept our eyes on your case." He said, "You accomplished a very big thing. And your husband's documents will be ready this afternoon at two o'clock." I thanked him for everything, and we left.

Now, I was starting to see that my husband was not able to go back to the United States until I came. When I asked my husband, "Let's start working on becoming an American citizen," his answer was, "I don't feel the need of it." He was so very wrong!

"Let's go find the TWA travel agency so we don't have to spend time looking for it. We still have money for lunch." We were enjoying our togetherness. It is amazing how awkward a person feels when the family is not together. We were having lunch. We needed to save money for the taxi to go to the airport. Soon it would be two o'clock.

"We should go back to the embassy for your documents."

They were already waiting for us. They gave us our necessary documents so my husband could live in America. It was very emotional. They wished us a very happy life in the United States.

We went to pick up our plane ticket and we would then be on our way to the airport. They said our plane would leave for London at five o'clock. We paid for our taxi. When we got to London Airport, they said we couldn't go further. TWA was striking! Wow! What would happen next? The airport personnel said we were going to get two hotel rooms, dinner, and breakfast. Then, the next day at eleven, they would put us on another airline.

We didn't mind it at all. The main thing was that we were together. We had dinner in a beautiful dinning room; first class everything! It was very nice to spend the evening in London. We telephoned Horvath and told him what time we would be in Washington and what time he should come to pick us up at the airport.

October 28, 1970, was a beautiful, sunny afternoon in Dulles Airport. A friend of ours, Horvath, was there to pick us up. We would stay with them a few days. The children right away wanted to go have a hamburger. But, the lady of the house would not allow it because she was going to cook supper. We reassured the children they would have a hamburger the next day.

Finally, it was morning, and we were going to Lila's. They were very happy we came back. It was very lucky we bought the car in Munich. That was how we were able to come back to America, with that money refunded for the price of the car. Lila said we still had eight hundred dollars from the car money.

That was the seventh miracle, that we purchased the car.

We rented an apartment. In three days, we could move in. We went to the bank. We needed money to buy a van. When the bank manager saw Laszlo, he asked, "Laszlo, my friend, how are you? Somebody told me you died. Where have you been?"

My husband said to him, "We went home."

He asked, "What can I do for you?"

My husband told him that he needed a vehicle.

The bank manager said, "Come into my office, and I will write you a check. Tell me, how many dollars do you need?"

With the check, we went right away to the Ford auto dealer and we drove out with a beautiful new, white, half-ton van! It was a good day.

The children had their hamburger. That was their lunch. All of us were very happy. I still had an old Sears credit card that we had got a long time ago. With the Sears card, we went to the store. We bought three beds, a kitchen table with four chairs, pots and pans, dishes; only those things most necessary so we could start all over our lives in America.

The next step was that Laszlo had to look up his customers. It is true, it was winter, but he liked to work for himself. Laszlo's customers loved his work. In the meantime, I took the children to school to sign them up.

I decided, since both of the children were in school, I would learn a trade. In case something happened to my husband, I could support the children. I decided I would be a cosmetologist.

We liked the apartment. In the apartment complex, there were about six hundred apartments. The owner and I became good friends, and Laszlo would be painting all of the apartments. In a big place like that, someone was always moving, and I would help him. The children were in school and we were working a lot. But, we didn't mind.

Freedom. What a tremendous word it is! Those who have lost their freedom, they know the meaning of that word and they value it.

For six weeks, I had been going to the cosmetology school. I liked it very much. I was glad I could go. I helped my husband a lot. I became a good painter. Since we were living in our apartment close to work, I was able to run home and put a chicken, stuffed chicken, pork chops, or steak or whatever into the oven. For one hour and a half, it was baking nicely in the oven. Then I ran back to work. After an hour and a half, I would tell my husband, "Dinner will be ready in a half an hour." He knew he should be home by then. I would go home to finish the dinner.

I would look into the oven, and uncover the meat. Oh, it was always beautiful! All it needed was browning. While the meat browned in the next half hour, I prepared the side dishes of mash potatoes, rice, or whatever. The children set the table. We opened a can of corn or green beans. I would tell the children that Daddy would be home in a minute. We sat at the dinner table, the four of us enjoying tremendously the dinner that I had prepared.

One day, my husband broke the silence. He said, "Elizabeth, how do you do that? You were with me working and we still have such a delicious dinner!

I said, "I carefully planned out my time."

The children left each morning for school with the seven-thirty bus. I started my cosmetology schooling at nine. Laszlo went on his way to his work. *By the way*, I think, *what should be the menu for tomorrow night?* We decided on stuffed chicken. Everyone agreed to it.

Victoria wanted to be called "Vickie." She complained that, in her bedroom, her side of the wall was very noisy. The neighbor girl played her radio very loudly. I reassured her that I would talk to them. They told us they would turn the radio off at ten, but they did not keep their word! I told Vickie we were saving our money to buy a house. She found a girl friend in the apartment complex, then she was happy.

The Szima family lived in Chicago. They wanted to move here to Virginia so they could be closer to us. That would be a problem, since Szima Alex didn't have any kind of trade and the wife didn't either. Where could we find a job for them? And, they also had a two year old little girl. We suggested they wait until spring time.

But a week later, they called us on the telephone. They let us know they had given up their jobs in the restaurant where they were working, and next week they were moving here and we should rent an apartment for them. My husband was very nervous. There were not that many jobs. We couldn't support them, too! I told him the problem will be solved somehow, since I believed in miracles.

We rented an apartment for the Szima family. My husband took him under his wing and taught him how to paint. After three months, Laszlo took my brother-in-law to his old friend, Mr. Brown, who owned a big painting company. Laszlo asked him to hire Mr. Szima, my brother-in-law, as a painter, so he wouldn't be disappointed in America. They had come to the United States a year ago. Laszlo reassured Mr. Brown that he would be a good worker. "I taught him!"

Mr. Brown said, "I will hire him, but just for you, Laszlo."

That's how, later on, Mr. Szima became a painting contractor. What was the thank you? His wife, Ilona, my sister, when we bought the house, said, "It's easy for you to buy a house since my husband worked for you."

I did not know what to say to her about that! So, therefore, I didn't say anything.

I put her into a free cosmetology school. That is how Ilona became a hairdresser. It was best to forget them. My husband worked hard and had a lot of customers. I finished with my cosmetology education. Already three or four shops wanted me to work for them.

Chapter 32

January 1973: We Bought a New House in America

In January 1973, we had saved up fifteen thousand dollars. I was on my way to find us a house. It seemed like the price of the houses was going up by the day.

One evening, the real estate agent called. She knew it was evening, but she wanted to show us a house in Greenbriar: four-bedroom, two-car garage, nice yard. She came to pick us up. She drove and drove. It seemed like we were going very far. Finally, we reached Greenbriar. Not bad! School was close. Hospital was close. Shopping center was close. The main highway to Washington and Maryland was close. It was true the house needed attention, but that was not a problem with us. The family decided we would buy it. The neighbors were young, like us, with children. Our kids would have a lot of friends. We put ten thousand dollars into the house. Two thousand dollars to sign the contract. All we had to borrow from the bank was thirty-five thousand dollars more. And, the bank loaned it to us.

We moved into the house at the end of February 1973. I wrote to Mother to get a passport. She was coming to America.

In May, she came. We were very happy for each other. Finally, she saw America and also where we lived. For her, too, it was a very big experience, seeing a black person the first time. She liked many things. She said it seemed to her that America had a democracy. She also said she had not seen so many ugly people in her whole life. She came for six months. We took her to a lot of places. We showed her the ocean. We enjoyed very much that she was with us.

The time came to say goodbye. My husband took her to New York. She had to change planes in New York. When she came, Laszlo went to

New York to help her change the plane. She told us how extremely nervous she was until the big door was opened and she saw Laszlo standing in the middle. "Oh, how relieved I was! Now I don't have to worry about getting lost."

We decided, with Laszlo, that we were going to bring out my twin sister and her husband, next. In the meantime, we got a letter. My twin sister was sick. The medications she required could be purchased in Germany. We right away took care of it and she got the medication. After all, she still needed surgery. The government sent her to Moscow. At that time, they did that type of surgery very well. My sister asked us to send them money, which was quite a lot of money, and we did.

My husband and I always helped anyone who asked. The newly immigrated Hungarians were all sent to us. I received a letter from my twin sister. The surgery was a success. She felt well, but the government had put her in a disabled retirement category. I felt very sorry for her since she was only thirty-six years old and she had to go to retirement. It hurts for such a young person and she loved company. She would miss the co-workers.

It was a beautiful spring in 1975. Greenbriar was such a nice place. Everyone had their property well taken car of. In our back yard, Laszlo made a beautiful patio. I put four big, beautiful, white wicker chairs there. I sewed nice, big, red pillows to put in. We had beautiful green grass, white chairs, with the red pillows and it looked like the Hungarian flag.

The children were in high school. My son was planning to join the Navy and he would be studying to be an air traffic controller. We were very happy but it was still four years away. Vickie was thinking to become a model and study fashion merchandising. Her father and I thought that was also very nice. In the meantime, we told them that, in that house, everybody had a responsibility. We were to provide, and they were to study well. They were good kids. They did not give us problems. But, of course, we were not our children's friends. But we were their parents. Everybody had to abide by the rules. Everyone was cared for and loved. Therefore, everyone was happy in our home.

My son was seventeen years old, and had his driving license. With his father, they purchased a very old car. It needed more oil than gas. But, it was good for a beginning.

In 1979, we invited my twin sister and her husband to America. They would arrive in May. My husband went to get them in New York. They were just as happy to see him as Mother had been when she came. We were very happy for each other. My husband took a semi-vacation. But they did go to work about four hours each day. He took my brother-in-law with him.

One day before they came home, my husband took my brother-in-law to the Landmark Shopping Center parking lot. He said to John, "You see that parking lot? Now, I will leave you here and I want you to count the number of parking spaces. I will be back in the morning to pick you up!"

Right away, he protested, "You are crazy!"

My husband said to him, "You remember in 1968 when we moved home and you were telling me about such a big parking lot in Moscow, even for thirty cars! Then, I said that was nothing, that in the United States, most parking lots have a couple of thousand parking spaces. I told you guys, and you called me a liar." Then Laszlo acted like he was going to step into the van and really leave him there.

Then my brother-in-law said, "I'm sorry, we didn't know!"

I have mentioned before that we lived in darkness under Communism.

We girls went shopping. We bought them a lot of presents, as we were trying to help them have a very memorable American trip. We made lots and lots of pictures. Shortly, it was time for them to go home. They said they had never had such a good time and that they were well taken care of. They would never, ever forget it.

In the fall 1979, my son, Laszlo, decided it was okay to call him Laszlo, since he found out from history books how many great men were called Laszlo.

The next morning, at six o'clock, we had to take him to the Fairfax Navy Recruitment place. We wouldn't be able to see each other for about six or eight weeks; until boot camp is over.

My little family was on the way to take my son. The distance was about twenty minutes. I was driving the car. Vickie and Laszlo were sitting in the back seat. My husband was next to me. The traffic was very light, since it was early morning. All of us were very quiet. My son broke the silence. "Mother, you are going to get a ticket for driving so slowly."

My thoughts were, *We are going to come back home without him. How are we going to get used to not having him at home with us?*

When we got there, we said our goodbyes with a lot of hugs and kisses. I asked my husband "Would you like to drive?"

"No, I will sit in the back with Vickie."

I drove, and realized that they were crying. I said, "You don't have to cry! People go away from other families, too."

Vickie said, "But, that is our family and there are just the four of us."

That was the truth.

When we got home, the house already seemed empty. I was thinking it would not be so easy. Everybody went to their work. Vickie still had two more years to finish high school.

At night time, there were only three of us at the dinner table. The family who always had a lot to say now was very quiet. I said, "We will get used to it. What is that, eight weeks? Then we are going to Chicago for the graduation."

We received a letter from Laszlo. Nervously, we opened the envelope. Everything was well. Laszlo would like to have a package. And he missed us, but he liked the Navy. We were relieved. I have to admit it; I missed him so much. I went up to his bedroom, looked around, and cried. I know only other mothers understand that.

We got ready to go to Chicago. We wanted to look very elegant. Vickie bought a beautiful white cashmere winter coat. I bought a beautiful fur coat. My husband looked like an admiral.

The day we left for Chicago, it was very cold. There was such a cold wind. We rented a car in the airport. We were on our way. We arrived at a large building.

We took our seats. The ceremony began. There came about eighty bald, young men dressed in black uniforms. They were so look-alike we couldn't find our boy. I am almost nervous. Vickie came. I asked her, "Have you seen your brother?"

She saw I was nervous. "Yes, yes! He is on the left side on the end."

Finally, the ceremony was over and we could see each other. Oh, we were so happy to see him. The eight weeks had seemed kind of long. We went to a restaurant for an early dinner. And we had the best Chicagoan Lasagna ever.

The next day, we went home to Virginia. Our son would be home for Christmas.

I received a letter from Mother. They were not as happy with the city living as I had hoped. They hardly tolerated each other. Father liked to go to the restaurant. He liked to bring his friends home. Mother wouldn't allow it. She said there was not going to be drinking in that house. Mother was satisfied with the family. She used to say, "We don't need strangers in our house."

But Father was very much in need of company. Mother sacrificed her whole life for her family. In spite of everything, they loved each other. But the lifestyles were very different. They argued a lot. I felt sorry for them. I think one of the problems was that they wanted more from their children than what they could give. Probably what they would have liked was that all of the children would be in their apartment much more than they were.

They were probably blaming each other. "Why don't they come to visit more?" They were working, and they had their own families. But, we don't know how short a time our parents have left on the earth.

A young man was interviewed on the TV. The question was, "Do you like your mother?" His answer was, "Yes, but not enough." It really got my attention. I loved my mother very, very, much. If I had known how orphaned I would feel when I didn't have her any more, I would have loved her more, too. But I did not know then that such a short time was left. I miss her very, very much. My beloved mother. To those who still have their mother, you need to love her. There is not much time left. Since they are the super glue in the family, no matter how old we are, we miss our mother's love terribly.

In 1981, Vickie finished her high school. We got ready to celebrate her graduation. She was sad that her brother could not come home from the Navy. We thought at that time that he had a girl friend. Vickie's graduation party was a big success. We had about forty young people. The party lasted until four in the morning.

Vickie went to work in the Hecht Company, in the high fashion department. She modeled the fur coats. It looked like Laszlo would not be an air traffic controller. He didn't like it any more. It was too stressful. I think he gave it up too soon.

Pretty soon, it was Easter. Laszlo would be coming home from the Navy. My brother would be here from Hungary. Ili sent him the plane ticket. We had a beautiful spring.

We got ready for the Easter holiday. I used to buy every grown-up an Easter bunny, and wrote their name on it. It didn't matter how old they were—twenty or thirty—everyone was very happy for their Easter bunny.

Vickie was dating. Her father said to her, "If a boy tries to behave badly, bring him home and I will knock him to the wall."

One day, Vickie brought home a young man. He must have been seven and a half feet tall. Vickie said to her father in Hungarian, laughingly, "Could you knock that to the wall, Daddy?" But we did not see the young man again.

When Christmas was coming, we always put up a beautiful Christmas tree. My son came home, too. They were getting ready to go to the New Year's Eve Ball.

The day after the ball, Vickie said she had met "Chip." "He looks exactly like Charlton Heston, the actor." Vickie always was in love with Charlton Heston. They started dating. Chip had a very dominating personality;

therefore, the dating has a problem. I saw my little girl was going to have a hard life with that man, and that is the way it was. But, love conquers all. Two years later, they got married on New Year's Eve.

My son finished the Navy life. We were sad that he did not learn a marketable trade. We are Europeans. It is very important that everyone have a marketable trade. He did become a very good electrician. Chip became a press mechanic. In four years in the Navy, he did not learn a useable trade, either. It looks like the four years spent in the Navy was not fruitful.

But, Laszlo did receive a medal for bravery when he saved his ship from a fire. He told us how the captain pinned the medal on his chest and he told us, and he told us. After a while, when he said, "Should I tell you how I received my medal?" everyone said, "No!"

My son brought a girl home. After about a year of dating, they got married. The marriage lasted two months. My son moved home. My daughter moved away. By the time my husband and I got used to the fact that now there were the two of us, then somebody moved back home. That was how it went for a while. I came to the conclusion that is where our gray hair came from.

My husband had a health problem. He didn't feel well. I sent him to the doctor. Dr. Gondor sent him to the cardiologist. After running tests, the cardiologist said, "Your husband has a small mitral valve problem."

I was just getting ready to go visit my parents in Hungary. When I talked to the doctor, I told him I would cancel my trip if my husband is in any danger. He reassured me it was not necessary. It was just a small problem. I should go and have a good time. He gave my husband a small white tablet. I don't even remember the name of it.

The days went by. Laszlo didn't have any particular health problem, except the kind when a very sexual man starts having problems with his heart. Since it was very new for him, he got to be very nervous. He started forcing the love making. But, he had to realize there was a problem. I suggested to him to go back to the doctor. When he came home, I asked what the doctor said. "Nothing. Nothing in particular."

In our bedroom, the only thing that happened was sleeping. My poor husband gave up even trying. In our bed, he stayed on the edge of the bed, like he was mad at me. I wanted to reassure him that we could be happy without sex. I loved him just the same. But his manhood was very much damaged. No matter how I hugged and kissed him, my husband was not happy. Quietly, we accepted present life.

We got news. Vickie and Chip were expecting a baby. We were happy for the news. It had been so long ago since we had had a baby in the house. Vickie was working for the government. Chip had a good job, too. They were saving their money. They wanted to buy a house before the baby came.

The money began to come together. They went out to find a house. "We found it! We found our house," she said. They were very happy. On the weekend, they were going to take her father and me to show us their house. We couldn't wait to se it. We were very interested to see what they bought.

Chapter 33

Vickie and Chip are Moving Away

Saturday morning, after breakfast, we were on our way to see the house that they had purchased. We were on the road about thirty minutes, then forty minutes. I asked, "Vickie, where is the house?"

She told me, "We will be there soon."

An hour later, driving eighty miles per hour, we finally got to the house. No neighbors nearby! Right away, I was thinking that my grandson would not have anyone to play with. And how would they come home in the winter time on that snowy, icy, curvy road? And it was very narrow, too. I have to tell you, we were flying at a high speed on that unpleasant, curvy road for twenty minutes. Then, I turned to my daughter, and I said to her, "I won't be able to drive that far and you know I don't like highway driving. In that case, I won't be able to help you with the baby and that makes me very unhappy."

My husband and I were very sad because she chose to move so far away from us. If we had any hair left which wasn't gray, it became gray, too.

Vickie said to her father, "You will paint the house, won't you, Daddy?"

He said, "Sure, my little girl."

In a few days, our disappointment eased. Vickie was six and a half months pregnant. We thought it best to start working on the house right away. Painting, wall papering . . . we had a lot of work to do on that house.

In March 1988, we had a beautiful spring. No matter which way you looked, you would see the spring flowers everywhere. The many different colors, and the azalea bushes! It seemed like they were in competition as to which one was prettier. And the fresh green grass! Everything was so beautiful. The cherry trees. You can't even imagine anything prettier than that.

God gave the humans such beautiful things to look at! I do hope everybody is happy.

Easter was coming soon. We were going to celebrate it in our house. The Szima family was coming, my son, Vickie and Chip, my husband and me – we were quite a few of us and we valued each other. Everyone enjoyed themselves. Since it was spring, my husband had a lot of work. Everyone was trying to beautify their houses at the same time. Since they liked his work, they would wait for their turn.

Saturday, we went to Vickie and Chip's house. We were making good progress with the painting. Vickie and I chose wallpaper and drapes, which I paid for. In about two or three weekends, the house would be ready. Everything would get done by the time the baby got here at the end of June. The master bedroom was completely done. The living room and dining room ceilings were done. We were thinking we would go home and continue with the paint job the next weekend.

As we were driving home, my husband said he was pretty tired. The next morning, I asked him, "Did you rest up?"

He said, "Yes, I feel fine."

Everyone went their own way. Laszlo Junior was an electrician. He liked his trade.

My husband said, "On the weekend when we go out to Vickie and Chip's house, there will not be much painting left to do."

I mentioned that there was still a lot of work to be done there, but, we said, "It will be done."

Chapter 34

April 28, 1988: My Husband, Laszlo, Dies

On Thursday, April 28, 1988, I was home, doing the house cleaning since, on the weekend, we would be at Vickie and Chip's house, painting. At three in the afternoon, my husband came home. We had a cup of coffee and we talked over the day's happenings. That took about a half an hour. He said he was going outside to look under the gutter. He thought some water had got under the siding.

"All right," I said. "In the meantime, I am going to finish the vacuum cleaning. All I have left is your office."

Our neighbor's fourteen-year-old son, Jack, was cutting our grass. Jack would finish the grass cutting pretty soon. I started to vacuum up the little office. I was hurrying because I needed to cook dinner. As I was vacuum cleaning, I heard a sound like when a sack of potatoes falls over. I thought that was strange. I would be finished in a minute, and then I planned to go take a look to see what that was.

In the meantime, I heard Jack calling my name. There was fright in his voice. "Mrs. Dobosi! Mrs. Dobosi!" I started running. We met at the sliding doors. Jack said to me, "Mr. Dobosi is lying there and not moving." He pointed at the big azalea bush.

I was about ten steps from him. I ran to my husband. I could see the white of his eyes; his tongue was swollen. I put my ear on his chest. It was completely silent. I told Jack to call the ambulance.

I could see the situation was very bad. I started yelling at my husband, "Laszlo! Get up! Get up! For God's sake, get up." But my partner in life was not moving.

The ambulance arrived. They pulled me off the ground. They moved my husband on the grass away from the bush. They tried to jump-start his heart. The chest jumped up. They were trying, again and again. In the meantime, two fire trucks came, and police people started asking questions. I was watching my husband. They wouldn't let me go close to him. Then they stuck something down his throat. By then, I was thinking, *Stop torturing him! He is dead.*

They put him into the ambulance. The police asked me where the children were. I gave Vickie's telephone number to them. "I don't know where my son works," I told them. I tried to find him on the telephone.

The telephone rang. Alex Szima was on the line. I said, "Alex, Laszlo died!"

He was shocked and said, "I will be right over."

The house was filled up with the neighbors. Everyone was crying. I was not crying. It could not be true, what had just happened here. But, what did happen? I didn't understand what had happened. It was unbelievable. Without him, there was no life.

My son came home. The policeman said, "Vickie is on her way to the hospital." Judy, my neighbor, offered to take me to the hospital.

We went to the hospital. The doctor came. He said he was very sorry, but Mr. Dobosi had died. In the meantime, Vickie arrived. They took us into a room. My husband was lying on the table. He looked like he was peacefully sleeping. The three of us stood next to the table with my husband on it. We tried to comprehend what had happened. But, that was not possible.

In the morning, everything was fine. We were standing next to the table with my dead husband on it. Nobody had died before, in our family. Why did he have to be the first one? There were so many things we wanted to do. Our first grandbaby was coming. We were waiting for him. I said to my children, "We should go home, I really don't feel good. In the morning, we will come back to Daddy." My poor things agreed to it. The shock was really, really, hard to take.

Vickie's husband, Chip, arrived. Alex, my brother-in-law, came. The neighbors brought dinner over. Next morning, the hospital called. Since the death was so unexpected, the law said they had to do an autopsy. I agreed to it. I wanted to find out why my husband died such a sudden way. After that, they were going to take his body to Fairfax, to the funeral home.

We had to go to the office to take care of the funeral arrangements. They were very kind. They acted like their own relative had died. We talked it over; what they were going to dress him in. I told them he was going to wear his smoking suit, his white ruffled shirt, his black bow tie, and shoes.

The man said I didn't need to bring the shoes. Oh, but I wanted him to have shoes. I knew he is going to heaven, but on the way, he needed shoes.

They said to me, "All right, bring the shoes. It is perfectly okay."

Next, we had to yet choose a coffin, the hardest job of all. We were taken into a room. My children were with me. There were a lot of coffins in that room. As I looked around, I saw Laszlo's coffin. It was silver gray. I made sure it was long enough and elegant enough to suit him. The whole thing took about a half a minute. It was such a painful experience, to choose the coffin for my beloved husband.

Then we were out of that room as fast as we could go. The viewing in the funeral home was going to be Saturday evening. And Monday would be the burial.

The Washington Hungarian Newspaper wrote:

Laszlo Dobosi—No More

Once more one of our valued members left our Club, who was supporting the Washington Hungarian's activities. Laszlo Dobosi, our friend, was born in Baja in 1928. The 1956 Revolution failed. He left his beloved country, Hungary, and lived in Virginia with his beloved wife, Erzsebet, and raised two children, Laszlo and Victoria. On April 28, Thursday afternoon, suddenly he died. His heart stopped beating. His sudden death shocked the Washington Hungarian community, all in sincere mourning.

His burial will be May 3, at the Virginia Chantilly Catholic Church. His family and friends will take him on his last journey. FMH lost it's most faithful member. With sincere sadness, we are saying goodbye to Laszlo Dobosi. We will cherish his memory. Rest in Peace.

On May 3, 1988, everything was taken care of. I had to be very careful. We couldn't forget anything. We could not re-do that. My husband's last journey on this earth had to be done with a lot of dignity.

We still had to go to the cemetery and pick out the burial plot. We were at the cemetery. Since it was at the end of April, the cherry and dogwood trees were in full bloom—pink and white. The cemetery looked so well taken care of and peaceful. It even had a fountain. The children and I decided that would be a nice, restful place for their father. The road separates the fountain from the burial site, and there is a little hill. As you look down towards the fountain, it seemed so peaceful. I asked the lady who was with us from the cemetery office if we could have that space.

"Yes"

"Then we would like that."

Alex called our friends. He let them know what happened, that Laszlo had died. Chip took care of the limousine. My sister, Ili, reappeared. I had not seen her for two years. We went home and a hot meal was waiting for us. I knew we had good neighbors, but such wonderful, caring, people they were. They divided among themselves, and every day someone came with a hot meal. But, Laszlo had always helped out everyone. He even shoveled the snow off the roof in the winter. We were good to all of our neighbors.

I could hardly wait for Saturday night. We were going to see my husband. We missed him terribly. We needed to see him.

Finally, it was Saturday evening, at six o'clock, and we were in the funeral home. Lots and lots of flowers were there. The casket was silver-gray and it looked very elegant. Everybody was there; all of our neighbors, friends, and customers. The big room was filled up with people. With my two children, I went up to the casket. We thought he would look like the way we left him at the hospital, peacefully sleeping. But that wasn't so. It showed he was dead. We were very surprised at the very big change in him. He was our first dead.

But the change was good. We could agree for him to be buried.

On May 3, 1988, Monday, at ten in the morning, he was taken to the Chantilly Catholic Church. I watched when his friends, with tearing eyes, put him on their shoulders, to take him into the church. The priest gave him a beautiful sermon for his last journey on earth.

Vickie went back to work. My husband's sister arrived from Hungary. She had missed her brother's funeral. After we picked her up at the Dulles Airport, right away she wanted to go to the cemetery where her brother was resting. Her name is Aranka. I put her up in Vickie's room. In the morning, I said to her, "Aranka, your brother was home during the night." I was very surprised when she said, "Yes, I know."

Aranka stayed for two weeks. Every day we went out to the cemetery. I needed to be near to my husband. I was suffering terribly. Before that, the way I was thinking, when somebody dies, the relatives are very sad, but I had no idea it goes with such physical pain. I felt like someone was cutting slashes in my body. The other thing I didn't understand, where all those tears came from. They were literally oozing out of my eyes by the bucketsful.

One of my husband's friends called me up and asked me how I was doing. I told him it hurt too much and I couldn't take it. He told me that, in eight months, it would be better. I asked him, "Are you sure?"

With his sad, quiet voice, he said, "Yes."

My sister-in-law's time was up and she left to go home to Hungary. I haven't seen her since!

Victoria's stomach was growing nicely. The baby was doing fine on the sonogram. We decided we had better finish the house painting that her father started because pretty soon the baby would be here. Finally, the painting was done. The paper hanging was done. There were drapes hanging on the windows. Vickie and Chip could move into their house. We said that her father would be proud of us.

June 1988 came soon. Since Vickie and Chip had bought a house so far away, it was very hard for Vickie, who was in late pregnancy, to drive that long way to work in Washington. Therefore, Vickie and Chip moved into Vickie's room. I was cooking dinners. And, I was going to the cemetery.

I tried to understand my life. I would stop in front of the mirror, and ask, "Who am I now? I am too young. I am fifty-one years old, but I am too old to start my life over again." The mirror didn't give me any answers. So, I said to myself, "Now, I had better go cook supper. My children will be home soon."

One early morning, I was sitting in the kitchen. I hadn't slept for weeks. When I fell asleep for a few minutes, I would dream of my husband. He would come and stroke me, trying to comfort me. I would wake up in my happiness, but he was not there. I would look at his empty pillow. Then, angrily, I would pull his pillow away. "You don't need a pillow. You are not here." Then I would go to the kitchen where the two of us always had our morning coffee and our talks. My husband always had either talked, told stories, or sang. We were never bored or lonely.

Chapter 35

1988: Vickie and Chip's Son is Born

One morning, at six o'clock, Vickie came down from upstairs. She told me, "Mother, the baby is coming. What should we do?"

Chip, her husband, was sitting at the top of the stairs. They were waiting for an answer from me. They saw they were not going to get much information from me, except to call the doctor.

The doctor said, "Come in to the office at eleven."

Vickie asked me, "Mother, what will happen to my birthday party dinner?" We called Vickie's mother-in-law. We told her there would not be any birthday dinner.

She said, "And why not?"

"The baby is coming!"

Vickie and Chip went to the doctor's office. Since Chip would be in the delivery room, she wouldn't need me. That is the style in America.

Laszlo came home from work at five. He said, "Mother, I am going to take a shower and change my clothes. Then we can go to the hospital."

We had just sat down in the waiting room and heard a loud sound. My son said to me, "Do you hear that, Mother? That was Vickie. That was her last push." A few minutes later, the nurse came to us. She said the baby had come and shortly we could come into the room and see them.

Everything was all right. What a relief! We were taken to the delivery room. Vickie was sitting in the bed with the baby in her arms. She said to me, "Look, Mother! See what we got."

I handed over a cream puff with one candle on the top. I told her, "Happy birthday, my little girl. What a beautiful birthday present you got!"

We got dressed in white hospital coats. In the meantime, Buck and Barbara, Chip's parents, arrived. The nurse handed me the new baby. As I was looking at him, I told my daughter, in Hungarian, "He is ours." I meant that he looked like us.

I didn't want to hurt Chip's parents' feelings; that is why I said it in Hungarian. When the baby was in Barbara's hands, she said, "That is a Hungarian baby." I have to admit it. I was happy he resembled our family.

I noticed Vickie was crying. I asked her why she was crying. She said, "Poor Daddy! How much he was waiting for his grandbaby and he will never be able to see my son."

I told her I was very sorry.

My sisters called me from Hungary. They told me my father was very ill and he was in the hospital. Since I wasn't able to say goodbye to my husband before he died, that bothered me very much. I right away bought a plane ticket so I could go and say goodbye to my father. When I arrived, the sad news was waiting for me. My father had died during the night. I felt I could not stand another funeral. Poor Mother, I was not in a condition to be able to help her, since I was a widow, too. Only two months ago, my husband had died. But she was lucky; her daughters were with her.

As soon as I got home, my first trip was to the cemetery. After I visited my husband's grave, I sat in my car. My eyes filled with tears. I thought, *I can not drive this way. I have to wait.* As I was sitting in the car, I noticed a strange sound. My car had a clock in it. My recollection was that that clock never, ever worked! On the clock, the hands were making the noise I had heard as they spun around. I thought, *That is not a coincidence.* I said to my husband, "You trying to tell me your time was up on earth?" A short while after that, the hands on the clock stopped.

That was the eighth miracle!

It had been six months since I became a widow. I walked through the house, from one room to the other. I was thinking that I had better figure out what I would do. I had no money because the income tax had just taken it all. On April 15, our bank account usually became empty. *Well, I* said to myself, *Elizabeth, you had better figure out something. My trade is not an easy one; I'm a hairdresser.*"

Four years ago, I had two herniated discs on my lower back. I remember when the doctor told us, "One is bad, but two are very bad." We didn't look on him kindly. He did mention that he was only a messenger. He was just telling us what I had. At a time like that, they say, a messenger gets shot.

I had the surgery. Seven months later, I was in a bad auto accident. Therefore, I have had many physical problems. I hired a lawyer and sued the woman who caused the accident.

In the meantime, I decided I was going to work from home. I would go into the hairdressing and alteration business, since my mother had taught us how to sew, too. I ordered two business cards. One said, "Betty does alterations." The other said, "Elizabeth does hairdressing." In a very short time, I was pretty well known, since my customers loved my work, and they recommended me to all of their friends and relatives.

I worked long hours. My son also lived with me. We got along very well. Vickie and the baby spent the weekends with us. The boy's name is Jerritt Janos. The neighbors visited often. My brother-in-law, Alex, and my sister, Ili come in my house and argue. They were living separately, then. They could not decide what to do.

One day, I told them, "You two should be ashamed of yourselves, coming here and arguing."

She said to me, "Oh, we are just taking your attention away from your sorrow."

That was all right because I could see there was a kind of courtship going on. But they weren't able to solve their problems. Therefore, they went their separate ways.

I had a few proposals, too. But, I decided I wouldn't get married, again. From the auto accident, I received twenty-six thousand dollars. It really helped me out a lot. Like they say, time heals.

At night time, my son and I would sit at the dinner table. My eyes would fill up with tears. My son asked me, "Mother, what does Daddy have to do with our having dinner?"

"Oh, but son, do you remember how much he used to love my cooking? And, he always told me at dinner, 'Honey, you are the best cook in the whole wide world.'"

"Yes, Mother, I remember."

"Now, you see."

My son dated now and then. I wished he would find his mate. Sometimes I saw loneliness on him. A very good wife was missing from his life. I was working way too much. I thought to myself, *Maybe I will move to Hungary.* After all, there was the apartment I had left for my parents in 1970. Since my father died, Mother hadn't wanted to live alone. She went to live with one of my sisters. I always thought that was a hasty decision. She gave up her independence very soon. I thought that, with the price of my house, I could live very comfortably with Mother.

My friend, Horvath, came from North Carolina. He was a widow. He wanted me to marry him. I told him, "I value your friendship tremendously, but we are just friends." I told Horvath, "Let's go to Washington to the Hungarian Embassy. I want to find out how I should go about moving to Hungary."

At the embassy, I told the ambassador of my intention. He was very nice. He said I would receive a counsel passport and I could come and go whenever I wished. I told him I intended to visit my children a lot. He said, "No problem. Anytime you wish."

I was very satisfied with the information. My friend, Horvath, said, "I will come to visit you in Hungary, too."

My days started at eight. The telephone would ring and they would ask for Elizabeth. I would know the phone call was for hairdressing, so I brought my hairdressing tools into my kitchen, where I did the hairdressing. And, when they called for Betty, I also knew that was for alterations. That is how I did things for four years. I didn't mind.

I learned that we were going to have another baby! Vickie was pregnant. I told my daughter, "Every mother needs a little girl." A lot of men, when they take a wife, they forget their mother.

Jessica was born, a very pretty little girl. She resembled the other side. I came to the hospital to visit Vickie and the new baby. Vickie was standing in front of the window where the nursery was, watching the babies. And she was crying very hard. I got very concerned. I asked my little girl, "What is the problem?"

She said to me "I am so happy she is a little girl. I don't have to go through that again." Vickie doesn't tolerate pain very well. Therefore, I understood why she was so happy for the little girl.

Chapter 36

October 26, 1991: I Met Don

In 1991, early spring, Shirley, my friend and customer, came for a haircut. She said, "My boss is a widower." Well, we discussed the widower; how tall he is, how old he is, does he have hair, how old is he, skinny or fat. Shirley said, "He looks very good."

Jokingly, I said to her, "Shirley, get me the widower." Then we laughed like young girls when they are talking about the boys. Don, the widower, wasn't mentioned again.

We had a beautiful spring. I had decided Alex should paint my house outside, since I like everything taken care of. The summer was very, very hot. I went to the cemetery. I was standing at my husband's grave, but it was so hot. Therefore, I decided to stay for only a short time.

One afternoon in October 1991, Shirley was on the telephone. She asked me, "Elizabeth, do you remember when we talked about the widower?"

I said, "Yes."

"I told him about you. He is asking for your telephone number. He would like to meet you. Can I give it to him?"

I said, "Yes."

We said goodbye. In a couple of minutes, the phone rang again. He introduced himself. "My name is Don Croll. Shirley mentioned me to you."

I said, "Yes."

Then he said, "I would like to meet you. Would Saturday be okay?"

"Yes."

Then he said, "I will pick you up at six."

I put down the telephone. I said to myself, *Wow! I agreed to meet that strange man!*

174

My neighbors came to visit. I told them, "I have a date for dinner on Saturday."

Right away they asked, "Who with?"

I told them, "With Don."

They said, "Tell us more."

"He is a widower and is Shirley's boss."

My neighbors were very happy.

"But, I don't think I am going."

All of them, at the same time, said, "And why not?"

"What am I going to do with a strange man?"

They said, "You are going to have dinner."

I told my children. They thought, too, that it was time to meet someone.

I thought, *Today is only Thursday. I have time to cancel that date.* I keep thinking, *I don't want to get married. On the other hand, it would be nice to have a man friend. After all, why am I sitting here, four and a half years all by myself?. I think I will keep the date.* I think I talked myself into it pretty well."

On Saturday, my neighbors came over. They wanted to be sure I would go on the date. At six o'clock, Don promptly arrived. In his hands was a small flower pot with a rusty-colored Chrysanthemum. It caught my eyes. since that is a cemetery flower. But I accepted it and I put it in the kitchen.

Don said, "Shall we go?"

"Yes."

He took me to the Hyatt Regency Hotel for dinner. Before we were taken to the table, the hostess asked, "Smoking or non-smoking."

Don, right away, answered, "Non-smoking." Don is very much against smoking and I was a smoker. After dinner, we went back to my house.

He told me he had become a widower a year ago. He also told me he had three children. I let him know I had become a widow four and a half years ago. He said, "Why didn't a pretty woman like you remarry?"

I told him, "That is not in my plans."

It was eleven o'clock, and time we said goodnight. As he walked toward the door, he stopped. With a firm decision, he asked me if I would see him again.

I thought, *What a decisive man! He asked me right here and now if I would see him again.* He did not leave wondering whether I would meet him again or not. Right there and then, he cleared it up. I really liked that in him. And I liked him otherwise, too: his height, his skin. He was not fat or skinny; he was good for me. So, therefore, I answered him, "Yes, I will see you again."

"Okay, then, I will come over Monday, after work," he said.

I remember I cooked supper. My son came home from work and they met.

Tuesday, after work, Don came. He said, "After supper, I will take you to my home. I will show you where I live."

I told my son, "I am going with Don."

He said, "All right, Mother."

At Don's home, we sat on the couch. We are realizing we were kissing. I said, "Oh, my! I didn't realize it was that late!"

Don said, "I will take you home in the morning."

I asked him, "You think so?"

He told me, "Yes, I will take you home in the morning." Don said, "Would you be my wife?"

I was very surprised. I told him, "We don't even know each other."

He said, "What I see, I like very much. And that is enough for me."

I didn't say anything. We had to think about it. We could hardly wait for it to be night time so we could see each other. It really seemed we were in love. Who would have thought, at our age, we could fall in love? I would have never thought.

One morning, while we were dressing, Don asked me, "When we get married, would you live in this house?"

Instantly, I thought, *A family grew up here—his family. Many, many, memories he has in that house.* I answered him, "Absolutely not."

He told me, right away, with a strong decision, "That is all right, we will buy a house for ourselves."

I have a nice house, too. I thought, *I don't think Don would like to live in my house either.* Therefore, I didn't ask him to do so.

We decided to sell the two houses and we would buy our own house so we could start our own new lives together. Don called his children to his house, two boys and a girl. Even the neighbor lady was there. He introduced me to them. Don's children were not thrilled about the news. Their sixty-year-old father wanted to get married!

Don's daughter, Nancy, said, "Why don't you two just date?"

Since we wanted to live together, we thought it was proper to get married. We decided we wanted to live together. Don's children were invited to my house, too, to meet Vickie and Laszlo. To look at them, it would have seemed a nice family together, five children, and grandchildren, too.

Don worshiped in the Methodist Church. He also sang in the choir. He asked me to go with him to the worship service on Sunday. We walked into the church and he sat me down, then went to join the choir. In the meantime, every Methodist woman had her eyes on me, and the men did, too. It seemed like the sermon was very long. Those women, Marilyn's friends, gave me the feeling, "Here is that hussy who came to town and took Marilyn's husband away."

After the sermon, Don introduced me to them. After the cold "Hellos," they turned away. I thought, *How un-intelligent they are. Their dear friend Marilyn must be ashamed of them. They should have been happy that Don found me. I am a good person, honest, and pretty good looking.* But, they didn't care about Don's interests.

In the meantime, Don and I were looking for a house or some condo. I asked my children what they thought about the whole thing. They told me I should plan my life in a way that was good for me. They said they liked Don. I told my children that I was very happy about that, because I liked Don, too, very much.

The holidays were coming. Don's work place had some office Christmas parties. He happily took me and proudly introduced me to everyone. I overheard the men talking. They were asking where Don found that pretty little woman. Somebody said, "Through his secretary. How lucky he is!"

In January 1992, we found a townhouse which we liked very much. That meant we had to put our two houses on the market. At the end of January, we called a real estate agent. We planned to get married after we sold the two houses because of the federal capital gains tax situation. My son got married. The real estate agent came ten in the morning. She put the for sale sign in the front yard. I thought it should take about eight to ten months to sell the house.

At the end of the street, the same house had been for sale about eight months. But, I couldn't believe what happened! At six in the evening, my real estate agent called and she said, "We have a contract on the house."

I told her, terrified, "No! No! No!"

But she said, "Yes! Yes!" That nice couple I brought over today is going to buy it.

I told her, "But I didn't think it would be sold that quickly!"

She said, "It seldom happens, but it happens."

On February 28, 1992, I had to move out of the house. If I would have cancelled, I would have had to pay the real estate person 6 percent of the price of the house. That is a lot of money. Also, if the contract purchasers sued, they could force the sale. So, I decided, since almost everything has a reason, I might as well go through with what we started.

The moving time came. Since Don's house had not sold yet, we moved all of my possessions into his house. In the meantime, our new house was getting built. When Don's house sold, we would be required to move into the new house. There was a contingency clause; it was required that both of our houses had to be sold by a certain date or the purchase contract would be null and void.

Chapter 37

1992: We Went to Scandinavia and Hungary

Every day, we waited for when a buyer would come for Don's house. Don saw that I was somewhat nervous. Nobody offered a price for the house. Don came home from work, and said he had an idea. A travel group was going to Europe—four countries for four weeks—and we should go with them. And by the time we came home, the house would probably be sold. It was a very good idea. We would go for another two weeks to see Mother. I could show him to my sisters and everybody. There were a lot of us for him to meet. I was very happy; I could hardly wait.

We planned to leave in April. Don said, "It is decided. I am going to take care of it."

I said, "And I am going shopping!"

Since we were going for six weeks, it was a long time. I telephoned Mother and the girls right away. They were very happy. They were eager to meet Don. We were going to Sweden, Denmark, Norway, Finland, and Hungary. We were going to see a whole lot. Don bought lots of film. He likes to take many pictures. I was going to leave that house just the way it was, since we were going to sell it anyway.

The next day, we left for our trip. We stopped in Budapest and visited my little sister, Juliska, since she lived there. We slept in the Liget Hotel. Don had already been in Budapest for a week when he traveled before.

Juliska, my sister, said, "It shows on you, that you are in love."

I told her it was a wonderful feeling. I would never have thought I would ever be in love again in my life.

Don said we would rent a car to go to Dunaujvaros. That is where all of my other relatives were living then. We just had to find the way out of Budapest.

I said, "How about if we hire a taxi to lead us out of the city? The rest will be easy." And that is what we did. Once we were out of the city, we paid the taxi man. He looked at us strangely. I thought, *Budapest streets are unknown for both of us and street names and route numbers are poorly marked or not marked at all. It would not make much sense to get lost for hours, since I can hardly wait to see Mother. We are making nice time going toward Dunaujvaros. We are going through many nice towns. Everywhere the spring flowers are blooming. The fragrance and the love I am feeling now is almost intoxicating. I am sorry not everybody is enjoying that wonderful feeling.* I told Don, "Here we are in Dunaujvaros."

We put our suitcases in the Gold Star Hotel. Then we went to my twin sister's house. We were very happy to see each other. Four years had passed since we had seen each other last. In the afternoon, we went to Rozsa's house. They had moved to Nagyvenyim. Mother lived with them. Everyone would be there. Anna asked me, "Is he the reason you didn't move home?"

"Yes, it happened at the last minute. I already had my papers to move home, then I met Don. That is how the plan was changed."

My twin sister said, "I am not surprised. He is a gentleman, and good looking, too. I am happy you like him."

"When are we leaving for Rozsa's house?"

"Right now," she said.

Nagyvenyim is a very pleasant town. It has pretty houses, lots of flowers in front of every house, and a very fancy iron fence in front of each house with different designs, and every one is painted different colors. They are very pretty.

It was new to Don. That was not the style in America. He was very busy taking pictures of them and the street. So, I urged him, "Come on! Come on! Mother is waiting and so are the girls. I can't wait to introduce you to them."

Finally, we stood in front of Mother. I saw on her that she liked Don, and the girls did, too. All of the relatives were at Rozsa's house. Rozsa cooked a big lunch for everyone. Her garden was filled up with spring flowers, fruit trees, and grape vineyards.

Josi told everyone how delicious the wine would be that year. But we couldn't forget Dino. Dino came with the house. He was the ugliest dog you ever saw in your life, and not very friendly. But he was nice to someone.

The girls noticed I was not smoking.

"Yes, but that has a story, too."

They asked, "What?"

"When I met Don, shortly after that, I realized he was very anti-smoking." When that came out of my mouth, my poor sisters almost choked on the smoke in their mouths. I remembered my husband, Laszlo, used to tell me, "Blow the smoke out; you are going to choke." Let's go back to my smoking. I was thinking it would not be pleasant to smoke around Don. Therefore, what would it be? Don or smoking? Well, I decided on Don. And, I also decided, starting today, no more smoking. That was six months ago.

My sister's said, "Wow! What a decision. Then tell us, do you cheat? Do you miss it?"

"I don't cheat, but miss it very, very much. But it will get easier. And it is worth it health-wise, too."

My poor sisters. From then on, they hid themselves with their cigarettes from Don.

I introduced Don to everyone. Mother told me she had a good place with Rozsa. Hedics Viki lives in Nagyvenyim, too, so, she has two daughters nearby. I showed Don, in Dunaujvaros, the Crooked Street where I lived when I lived there the first time, in 1952, when I got to Dunaujvaros. I also showed him the Petofi Park. Anna and I lived there. Later, my husband and I, when we were newlyweds, lived there. That was the year I was the happiest in my whole life. One terrible day, everything changed.

I told Don, "Tomorrow we are going to the farmer's market." Dunaujvaros had a very big and wonderful farmer's market. I knew Don liked these things. "We shouldn't forget the beautiful Danube, too. As you stand on the plateau, you can see far, far away, to very pretty scenery. And if you get tired, there are nice benches where you can sit down and rest. In the park are lots and lots of works of art—statues. Some of them you don't know what the artist was trying to say. But, each of them is very entertaining and interesting."

There was a museum showing the beginning of Dunaujvaros. The story was very short, and looked like the person who put it together didn't know very much about that era. For sure, the person who put it together wasn't there in Dunaujvaros at that time. It would deserve much more detail. Dunaujvaros' past changed many, many men and women's lives.

Quickly, our time was gone in Dunaujvaros. We were on our way to Copenhagen. We had to say goodbye to everyone. I was very happy I had been able to see Mother and everybody. Don made lots and lots of pictures. In one of the pictures, there were twenty-nine of us. And since then, the family has grown. That is what I missed very much in America.

We met our travel group, twenty-five of them, in Copenhagen. When we settled down in our comfortable tour bus, our tour director said to us, "Please don't fall asleep before I let you know the rest of the day's program."

Most of us asked him, "You mean people fall asleep on the bus?"

Laughing, he said, "As soon as they put their butts in their seats."

Shortly after that, we realized he was telling the truth. We could hardly hold our eyes open. In the evening, we stopped in front of a very nice hotel. By then, we had pretty much got to know our travel partners. Our tour director was a pleasant young gentleman, as was the driver. It looked like we were going to have a very pleasant four weeks.

The scenery was beautiful. Our hotel rooms were also very comfortable. After dinner, our tour director asked for our attention. He said, "In the morning at six o'clock, the suitcases should be out in the hallway."

Everybody, at the same time said, "Six o'clock?"

His answer was, "Those who wish to sleep should not come on the trip."

After that, nobody said a word, no matter how early we had to put the suitcases in the hallway.

The next morning, after breakfast, we traveled through Denmark. We were in that beautiful little town, the home of Hans Christian Andersen. The gigantic tour bus practically was driving with one wheel on the sidewalk since the street was so narrow. It had well-taken-care-of, beautiful little houses. Flowers were everywhere, just like we used to see it in the children's story books.

I had a guilty conscience. I was so worried that the big bus was going to damage the beautiful little houses. Oh, I was so relieved once we were out of the street.

We were traveling along, and as far as our eye could see, there were yellow flowers. What scenery! Somebody said, "Those are not flowers, those are rape. They make canola oil out of the rape seeds." They were flowers and beautiful. Don took pictures from the bus. If there was nothing to take pictures of, then we were kissing. We didn't have much to talk about since we had no past together. I thought, *Not to worry, we will create our own past.*

In Norway, we saw a lot of castles. If you ask me, too many! There were also lots of churches. They were mostly with dark interiors. Many, many tunnels were there to drive through. We saw lots and lots of mountain sides that looked like they were decorated with rare jewels where the stones sparkled when the sun shined on them. We also saw a lot of water falls. They were oozing down from the mountain sides like liquid diamonds. I couldn't take my eyes off them.

I thought, *How much God loves us, to create such beauty for mankind!*

The next country was Sweden. We went to Stockholm on a very comfortable Globus Tour bus. Right away, we were looking for the blue eyed, blond haired people. But we couldn't find them. We saw the building where they gave out the Nobel Prize. When we went into the building, in one room, there were large tapestries hanging on the wall, with Sweden's history on them. There were many castles and palaces.

From Stockholm, on the ferry, we went to Helsinki. When we stood near the ferry, I was amazed they called it a ferry. The ferries I had seen in my life could fit two cars and a few people. This ferry looked like a city. It held, not only 1,500 cars, buses, and trucks, but also banks, stores, restaurants, casino, a swimming pool, elevators, and more. I couldn't get over how gigantic that man-made floating city was. After dinner, we looked at everything, and checked out everything.

We decided to go to bed. We looked at the narrow beds. It is amazing, when two people are in love, how small a space they can fit into. The Baltic Sea was quiet and peaceful. Just like us, after beautiful love making.

After a peaceful night, we awoke rested. Don said, "Let's go and have breakfast. I would like to check that ferry over once more." We were on it until one o'clock that the afternoon. The ferry's name was *Symphony*. Since I was not fond of massive water, I was happy to leave that magnificent, floating city.

From Helsinki, we flew to Rovanimi, Lapland. When we went into the hotel, we saw that every window was covered with black drapes. The reason for that was because, day and night, it was daylight above the Arctic Circle. I would not like to live there. I like it very much when the night is dark.

I have to tell you that, here, for the first time in my life, I sat on Santa Claus' lap. He had the most beautiful blue eyes. I asked him if I was too heavy. He said, "Not at all. You can sit here all day."

After two more days, we left for home. We were hoping to have a buyer for our house.

When we got home, Don went back to work. My little girl came to visit, with her little children. We have never been apart so long from each other before. We were very happy to see each other. She said, "I see the house hasn't sold yet."

I said, "The way it is, we don't have offers for it."

Don went to work. I was practically in a stalemate position. I was in the house, going from room to room. I looked at it. What a well-designed house it was! I thought, *I could make a beautiful house out of that. It would be a sin to waste it.*

I could hardly wait for Don to come home from work. I greeted him. "I have an idea."

"Do tell; I am interested."

"Since we don't have a proper offer for the house, if I could decorate it to my taste, I would not mind living here."

Don said, "I want to live where you live. You can do what ever you want with the house." Don said, "We are going to take it off of the market. I will call the real estate agent."

The next day, I began to plan. I wrote down the wall colors. We would pick up the twenty-year-old carpet, get a new kitchen floor, new lights, wallpaper some walls, and sand the hardwood floor. Four of the five bedrooms and two of the three bathrooms were upstairs.

I told Don, "I am going to make a beautiful office out of one bedroom for you." That way, he wouldn't have to be in the basement, because that is where the computer was at the time.

He was happy for it. I was happy, too. I would have a lot of work to do and I loved to decorate. I could already see how beautiful that house would be when I finished with it.

Don said, "Then we can get married! What do you think about in two weeks? On July 11?"

So we agreed on it. It seemed to me that Don was happy. He called his children, but they were not happy we were staying in the house. They also were not happy about us getting married. I was sorry, but we were not talking about their futures. They acted jealous and unfriendly toward my children. What luck they were grown up, and didn't need to see each other.

I was very happy. My children saw that I liked Don. They accepted him and they were very nice to him.

Chapter 38

July 11, 1992: I Married Don

July 11, 1992, was the wedding day. My son walked me down the aisle to the minister. He was very proud. We had a holiday-like atmosphere in our wedding. The immediate family was invited, and Shirley, Don's secretary, who introduced us to each other. We had lunch at the Hyatt Regency Hotel where we had our first date. Everybody enjoyed themselves. Maybe, Don's children did, too.

The new week started and everyone went home. Don went back to work. I was there in the house. I believed we needed to start out in one room and go from there. It looked like, in the last fifty years, nothing had been thrown out.

One evening, Don was taking care of the bills on the computer. The computer was in the basement, one level down from the laundry room. The laundry room had many cabinets and closets. I decided to work in the laundry room that night, so I would be near to Don. As I was checking out the cabinets and cleaning them out, on the top shelf, I found a box. "Marilyn" was written on it.

I went to Don and I said, "Look, Marilyn got a package."

Don said to me, "Elizabeth, please sit down." There was a chair and I sat down on it with the cardboard box in my lap. Don looked at me with worried eyes.

I asked, him "What is the matter?"

He said, "Elizabeth, it is not a box. That is Marilyn's ashes."

I asked, "Why is it in the box?"

He said, "I didn't know what to do. You will help, won't you?"

We decided that, the next day, we would buy a pretty urn. The place in the cemetery where Laszlo was buried was a pretty place. So, with dignity, we would put her ashes into a columbarium. Then, if her children wished to talk with their mother and take her flowers, they would have a place to go.

Don was very happy. He looked at the box still sitting in my lap. I said, "Then, I will take it upstairs and put it in the room. Tomorrow we are going to the cemetery to buy a columbarium niche."

Everything went nice and smooth. Marilyn went to the beautiful cemetery from the laundry room. Her children were very happy. One of her best neighbors said to me, "Thank you, Elizabeth, thank you."

I went to work on the house. The junk went into the trash. I called the painter. I planned to wallpaper the three bathrooms. My son, Laszlo, was going to put up the new lights, since he was the best electrician. We made such progress with the house. We bought silk, hand-woven Chinese rugs. The furniture from our two houses, I divided up in that big house. It was very elegant and pretty. Don was very happy about it. But, we still had a lot to do. Of course, the yard was a lot of work.

In the neighborhood, I met Istvan and Julia. One of my neighbors had given me their address. One afternoon, I decided to look them up. Around their patio, there was a wooden fence, painted red, white, and green. I knew right away that I was at the right house, since those are the Hungarian flag colors. When I rang the bell, Istvan opened the door. I said in Hungarian, "Good day!" Istvan showed on his face a pleasant surprise. I told him I lived on the other side of the park. Julia came back from her afternoon bicycle riding. She was very happy to see me, too. We Hungarians in foreign lands are very happy to see each other. And we became good friends, too.

Now, back to the house. I continued my work. In January, Don would have a birthday. I thought I would give him a big birthday party. I asked him about it, and he seemed to be happy for it, too. I was also happy, for I had a lot of work to do.

We paid off Don's house. My name was put on the deed. Therefore, the house belonged to both of us. But, I was not feeling myself at home. I felt myself homeless and poor. The only way I could get away from that feeling was if I didn't give myself time to think about my life. I told that feeling to my sister, Maria.

She said to me, "I know exactly what you are talking about. That is the way I was when we moved into my second husband's apartment."

But her six-year-old little girl said to her, "Mother, let's act like we always lived here."

I thought what a smart little six-year-old girl that Erika was! Too bad I did not know that. It would have saved me a lot of grief.

Don's son called him over one night. He accused him of not being a good grandfather to their little girl. He didn't go to their house to take her for a walk. And he wasn't a good father, either. Tom was very critical of his father. It didn't count that his father worked hard for a living and his mother was able to stay home to care for the three children. It is really interesting that some of our children—it doesn't matter how old they are—are still looking to see if we give them enough. Too bad it doesn't occur to them that it is their turn to give.

Of Don's three children, I did not notice any caring toward him. It was not hard for me to see they were cold and uncaring, but I was not going to allow them to decide my happiness, since that would be up to Don, anyway.

We were making progress with the house decoration. Shortly, Don's birthday would arrive. He would be sixty-one years old. We invited his co-workers and everyone from the neighborhood. Don's son, Tom, said they were not coming. They had a previous engagement to go to.

I said to him, "On your father's birthday?"

He said, "No big deal. We can celebrate it another time."

I told him, "Well, you knew it."

The party was pretty flat with the Coca-Cola and soda water, since Don is anti-alcoholic.

Chapter 39

November 2000: Widowed Twins Face Life

Two years ago, my brother-in-law, my twin sister's husband, suffered with stomach cancer. Surgery was not an option. Therefore, his life on earth would be short. Hard days were ahead for my poor sister. In my absence, I tried to help financially. Before I put a hundred dollars in an envelope, I put it in a piece of a newspaper so it wouldn't be seen through the envelope. The doctor cost a lot of money, since in Hungary it was the practice to show gratitude to the doctors with money. That came to be a practice a long time ago. The patient and the family felt they would get better care if they showed their appreciation to the doctor with money. When a patient was ill for a long time, the appreciation money really added up to thousands.

My brother-in-law, after a long illness, said goodbye to his earthly life. Now, my poor sister holds the rank of widowhood. I am truly sorry for her, since I know how sad it is to lose our partners in life. With his sudden death, I wasn't able to go to the funeral.

In the beginning of November 2000, I was on my way as an experienced widow. I was hoping I would be helpful to her. It seemed like she was happy I came. She was left with a very small retirement. With my saved-up money, we shopped for what she needed. I felt only I was able to do that for her. Her children were raising their young families. In the meanwhile, I noticed how differently we were handling our sorrow. When I became a widow, I went to the cemetery and argued with my husband, "Why did you die? Why did you leave me?" I could not handle the facts of life.

But, my sister went into the pantry. She worked in there for hours. She said, "I am taking everything out to the trash." And she did. I tried to not be in her way.

Don came for Christmas. I remember we put up a tiny little Christmas tree. There were just the three of us. I painted the frame of a painting that Don brought me from home with gold paint.

That Christmas Eve, that was how it was. My brother-in-law was missing from the apartment. He had been like my husband. He filled up the room wherever he was. After their deaths, the get-togethers really got flat. I remember, in our younger times, we used to laugh until our faces were hurting.

Anna's son and his wife, Gabi, had invited us for Christmas lunch. It was a very pleasant day. After the Christmas holiday, we were going to Budapest to my sister, Juliska, and her husband's. We planned to spend a week with them. Lajos and Juliska had already bought the New Year's Gala tickets. That would be a beautiful evening, with a lot of entertainment. Don liked it very much, too, in spite of the fact that he didn't speak the Hungarian language.

In Budapest, we liked to go to the Café Gerbeaud's famous coffee house. We liked it there very much. We shouldn't forget the Budapest Circus. Every time we went, we saw an excellent circus. For Christmas, Juliska and I received beautiful fur coats. Lajos received a new TV. Santa Claus was very good to us. Juliska thanked Don for her fur coat, very much. Lajos, the husband, got jealous. We took it as being childish. Don and I liked my little sister, Juliska, very much.

Oh, how sad we were when we found out she had lung cancer. Poor little Juliska, after two years of suffering, she died. Now, we had had six deaths in our family. After Juliska's illness, everything pleasant changed. How much one person's presence counts! If some person was and then was no more, they said it didn't stir up a lot of water. Our Juliska was a small person, not quite five feet tall, but she really lit up a room. She was kind and loveable, and she loved life. I hoped that, in heaven, she would be happier than during her earthly time.

Chapter 40

July 16, 2001: We Went to Transylvania

Parc Laci, my brother-in-law, Magdi's husband, told me on the telephone that they thought it would be nice to go to Transylvania and visit my birth place. I was very happy. I hadn't seen my birth place since 1942. I was so excited! Laci said there would be eighteen of us. They would rent a small bus, a trailer for the luggage, and hire a driver and a tour director.

"It sounds very good. When are we going?"

He said, "July 16, 2001."

"Please sign us up. too," I told him. "Don and Elizabeth." I told my brother-in-law, who was organizing the trip, "Tomorrow, we are going to take care of the plane tickets. Just like you said, sixteen of us are going from the family. How very exciting! I hardly can wait."

Don and I flew to Hungary. The day of our Transylvanian trip arrived. We stood in front of a restaurant, waiting for our tour bus. I looked over at my sisters and their husbands. Magdi brought their two children, Andrea and Laci, Jr. Julia brought their only son, Lolika.

My twin sister, Anna, said, "It is too bad our poor brother is not alive. He would have come, too.

I have to be honest, I would have never dreamed of such a trip. I was most interested in our birth place, and our house. The big picture window. My memory of when Anna and I were throwing the rock to the roof and I told Mother, "Anna's rock hit the window." I wanted to see that window.

I remembered our beautiful Easter. And that was the house where the angel brought in the Christmas tree. That was where our mother baked delicious pastries for Christmas. There, in that house, the ice sickles hung from the gutter. That was where the three of us, from that window, watched

Mother when she took the Easter basket food to the church so the priest could bless it. The basket was covered with a beautiful, white cloth. Uncle Steve came and brought us writing papers and fancy pencils. These were the things I would like to see, again. These were my beautiful memories.

The bus arrived, and we were so very happy that the family was traveling together. Eight days would go fast! At the Hungarian / Rumanian border, it took a long time to cross. Finally, we are on our way. The roads in Transylvania were pretty much neglected. We stopped at Nagyszalontan and visited the Arany Janos Museum. When the museum curator found out Don was from America, he said, "Just a minute! I will be right back. I am going to bring something." It took him about a minute or so. When he came back, in his hand, he held an American Constitution. He proudly showed it to Don. Don was really moved.

Since our tour director was a professor, he wanted to teach us the two-thousand year history of the country. We were moaning; we were not school kids. We wanted to see where we were going. We wanted to see the scenery and we also wanted to talk about it.

What is the lesson from that? You don't hire a university professor for a tour director.

We saw all of the beautiful sights. Finally, we reached our birth place, Csik County, town of Gyergyoalfalu, The rain was coming down in buckets. We decided to go into the church where we had been baptized. Anna and I knelt in front of the altar.

Don tried to take a lot of pictures inside the church. His main 35 mm camera would not work in the church. He had been taking pictures outside the church! He tried new batteries. The camera still wouldn't work. He got his back-up 35 mm camera and it would not work, with two different sets of batteries! Right after that, both cameras worked fine outside the church!

As of today, we still do not understand why both of the cameras failed to work and we ended up with no pictures inside the church. All of the other pictures turned out fine.

We started out to our street. It was still raining hard, but we were on our way to find our house. We looked into houses and we told people we were the Kerteszs and we were looking for our birth house. Since the residents of the street had mostly changed, they said, "Sorry, but we don't know where that house is."

With my twin sister, we went ahead. The rain was still pouring down. We said, "That is the street; our house has to be here. We have to find it." We went ahead in that terrible rain. We were almost at the end of the street. It was really lightning. They say our town is famous for the most deadly lightning strikes.

An old couple came down the street. They could see we were strangers in the town. They asked us, "Where are you going?"

My sister and I said, "We are looking for the Kertesz house."

"Oh," they said. "They tore it down a long time ago."

I asked, "They tore it down? That is too bad. We won't be able to see our birth house. We have to be satisfied with our sweet memories of it."

The professor left us only a short time in our town. He said, "We should be on our way." From my perspective, our birth town was the most important part of that trip, probably because my brother, Anna, Maria, Julia, and I were all born here.

We traveled from city to city. We enjoyed the beautiful, Transylvanian scenery. Since the roads were in quite bad shape, something went wrong with our bus. Shortly after, the bus stopped. The driver checked it over. In the meantime, we went to lunch. We saw the driver coming. We all asked him. "What is the problem with the bus?"

He said, "It is a small problem." He said, "We can go on ahead and I will fix it tonight."

We said, "How can we go ahead? It is making a terrible, loud noise."

He said, "It is not dangerous. And we have to go back to the hotel." We were about a two hours' drive away. Finally, we arrived at the hotel. We could hardly wait to get out of that horribly noisy bus.

When we were coming down a steep decline, I looked into the forest on the side of the road. I was hoping we wouldn't wind up in there. Sixteen of us in that bus from our family, plus the professor and the driver; it would be a terrible loss to our family if all of us got killed. But, God was with us.

We got back to the Jakab Antal house. That was where we had our rooms, and where we got our breakfast and suppers. It was a pleasant place.

We spent our last night in Transylvania in the Dacia Hotel. It was a pretty nasty place. My poor twin came from her room. She said, "Please let me sleep with you. I am afraid in my room."

Of course, we had single beds; one for Don and one for me. I told her, "Come on. We will share my bed. There will be enough room." That is how we slept our last night in Transylvania.

We were on our way home. At the border, there were many trucks and cars waiting to get through. I held a very pleasant memory in my heart of our Transylvania trip. In a few days, Don and I were going home to America. My son and my daughter, the grandchildren, and friends were probably all waiting for us. I began to miss them.

Chapter 41

Life With Don

Don and I arrived at our home in Fairfax, Virginia. I would like to discuss my life with Don. Don created himself a world with very thick walls which could not be entered easily. It seemed like he felt good in it. That became obvious when, suddenly, he went to retire. Both of our lives changed tremendously after he began to stay home. It came to my attention how private a person he was. I had a hard time with that, because my first husband was always telling stories and singing. With him, there was no loneliness. With him, life had meaning. I felt very needed and wanted with him. He used to tell me, "Without you, there would not be life."

Don wouldn't say anything for hours. He gave me a feeling like, "It is okay that you exist, but without you, it would not be a problem, either." It was important for Don to have a wife, just to have a wife. Everybody must be needed and wanted. That is important for our emotional health.

I have a very sweet story. I saw it on the TV. The aunt was the housekeeper for her nephew where there was an eight-year-old little boy. The aunt went away to visit her sister for a week. When she came home, of course, the house was a mess. She told them what pigs they were. A few months go by, and the Aunt is on her way to visit her sister, again. Her nephew hired two women from the town to clean the house before his aunt got home. They waited for her with a clean house. The time came, and it was ten minutes before the aunt would be home. The father and son proudly looked at the neat and clean house. The boy said, "Father, Aunt Rosie will be very surprised. She will see we don't even need her." The father said to his son, "What did you say?" He repeated, "Aunt Rosie will see she is not needed at all." The father looked at his watch. Ten minutes and Aunt Rosie would be here. He turned to his son and said, "Let's hurry and make as big a mess as fast as possible." The boy looked with wide open eyes, but the father said,

"Hurry up! Hurry up! Don't forget to put a peanut butter sandwich under your pillow." Just as soon as they finished tearing the house up, the door opened. Aunt Rosie was home. As soon as she was in the house, she looked around. With happiness in her eyes and a smile on her face, happily, she started scolding them. "What pigs you two are!" The father and son stood there, looking guilty and sorry, and promised the next time they would be more careful and not make such a mess, either.

Aunt Rosie would have been terribly sad if she had found a clean house. I am sure she would have thought she was not needed. That is the way we are. We need to be needed. Life is empty, otherwise. I am sorry to say that is how I felt with Don. He never told me no. He was just that way. I told him, sometimes, "Who doesn't give of himself won't receive, either.

We traveled a lot with about twenty-five other people, mainly married couples. When we stopped with the bus to look at a city, Don would run around by himself, as he wanted to take pictures of everything. The other men were hand-holding with their wives and watching the city. They were sharing their experience. In the meantime, I was also city watching, but by myself. I had no one to discuss my opinions with.

One time, we were getting ready for a trip. We were in a store shopping. I looked into our shopping cart. I asked Don, "How many rolls of film do you have in there?"

He said, "Eighty-six."

I said, "Isn't that a lot?"

He said, "Oh no."

I said, "You don't have to take a picture of every fly."

He said, "You are going to choose which one I am going to take a picture of."

The breakfast wasn't any better. While other people were eating their breakfasts, Don told stories to them; therefore, we were almost every time the last couple to get on the bus.

The dinner was played in a similar way. When we were traveling to Hungary, after we had boarded on the plane, Don went to use the restroom. Finally, a half hour later, he came back. He pointed to other side of the plane, where a Canadian woman was sitting, and told me that was where he was going to be, so I shouldn't worry. Then he turned around, and he left. He went back and sat with the Canadian woman. That is where he sat until Frankfort, where we had to change planes.

In the meantime, all by myself, I sat on the other side of the plane. When we got off the plane, Don said goodbye to the woman. "Goodbye, Canada! Goodbye, Canada!" Don wasn't bothered by the fact I was sitting in my seat all by myself for eight hours. I did not understand that, not at all, especially, since the man had three degrees.

He had more strange things like that at other times, too. We had been married for eight years and sometimes the loneliness was unbearable. I had neck surgery which turned out pretty badly. Therefore, keeping a big house clean had become a struggle. We were thinking about a smaller place to live. One day, I came home from shopping. Don greeted me. He said, "I have a very good idea."

"Well, please tell me; I am interested."

To my very big surprise, he said, "We should move to Hungary."

I couldn't believe my ears. "You are joking, aren't you?"

Don said, "No, I am not. You would be with your twin sister and the other sisters. You miss them anyway."

"But, you don't speak Hungarian. What would you do?"

He said, "I will learn. You resent that I spend so much time on the computer, anyway. You will go to your sisters and you won't be lonely." He said, "That will be good for both of us."

I said, "I hope you realize the lifestyle is very different over there."

Don said, "Of course I do. We have been going over there the past eight years."

"Then you won't mind living there?"

"Oh, no. I like it there."

I started thinking about it. Don mostly thinks of himself 80 percent of the day, sitting in the office. At night, we watch TV. Then we go to bed. If I don't come up with some sort of subject, then we didn't have any conversation. I can't get used to it. The whole quietness is very irritating to me. I was starting to forget the Hungarian songs that my husband used to sing to me. In that quietness, I felt terribly lonely. I felt like Don and I didn't have any common interests. I thought about his idea. After all, his children and he were not talking. He sat in his room ten hours a day. It really didn't matter where and what room he sat in.

My children could come and visit. And I would be with my sisters. Especially, with my twin sister. One time, my twin sister said to me, "When we are retired, I am going to live in Dunaujvaros." Then she told her little story. When she worked in the coffee shop, she had two elderly woman customers. They showed up every day. They sat down to the table. They ordered a small coffee for the two of them, with an extra cup. They wanted to divide it fairly. They kept pouring the coffee into the cups and they wound up losing half of it on the table. And these two old ladies did that every day. I imagined that little story with ourselves in it.

When Don said we could move to Hungary, to Dunaujvaros, right away that little story came into my mind. *My God!* I thought. *It will come true what I imagined so many times.* I can already see us dressed up and going to the coffee house.

Right away, I went to Don. I asked him, "Please examine your idea very carefully and if you could live in Hungary, then I would like to move there."

Don said, "Why not?"

Well, then, it was decided. And he started with a plan. We were going to buy two apartments, side by side, and make one big apartment out of it. It sounds good, doesn't it? Then I would talk to my son and my daughter to see what they thought about the whole idea.

Vickie said, "I will miss you, but I know your life is lonely here. If you think that is what you want, that is okay with me. We will come to visit, and you can come visit, too."

"Then it is okay?"

"Yes, Mother."

My son came. I reminded him that he knew we were looking for a smaller home.

"Yes, Mother."

"We were thinking to go to Hungary."

He said, "What? And Don?"

I said to him. "It is Don's idea."

He looked at Don. "Is that the truth, Don?"

Don said, "Yes. I like it there."

My son said, "It sounds like you have already decided." I have to mention my son has a very unpleasant memory about Hungary when we lived there in the '70s. And he does not forgive easily. "Mother, I am going home. I am going to think about all of that."

I told him, "All right."

The next day, my son came. He said, "If that is what you want, it will be good for you there. I know, Mother, you have a lot of relatives and sisters. Then you two can come and visit." Then he asked, "Over there, it is not like in the '70's, is it?"

"Oh, no. It is all different—for the better." We looked at each other, with Don, and we thought that was settled.

Next, we went to the Hungarian Embassy in Washington to see what we had to do. In the embassy, the ambassador informed us how we should go about it and he did not see a problem, since Don had a Hungarian wife. And we were given a lot of documents to fill out. When we got every document completed, we should bring them back and, in three or four months, we should receive permission to live in Hungary.

Next, I had to call my twin sister and tell her the plan. First, she was surprised. I didn't blame her. It was such big news. I said to her, "Imagine we are going to the coffee house just like those two other ladies." She had forgotten the story. I reminded her of those two ladies who divided the one small coffee between them.

"Gee, you still remember that story?"

"Of course, that is what you said we would do, too." That little story was deep in my heart, always and it looked like it is going to come true.

"Now, how can I help?"

"Would you please find two apartments, side by side, and then buy them. The most important thing is that it they have to be in the center of the city so we will be close to each other. You don't have to hurry. Take your time.

My twin sister said, "I will be very happy to help. You did so many good things for me." Both of us were very happy.

She looked at many apartments. Then she found two apartments, side by side. In the meantime, we were sending the money.

"Go ahead and buy them. In the fall, we will come and we will take a look at them." "How far are they from you?"

She said "Eight minutes. We will be eight minutes from each other. I timed it on my watch."

"Wonderful, absolutely wonderful."

In the fall, we were in Dunaujvaros. My nephew, John, found a contractor who would do the renovations on the apartments. Don made a drawing of how the apartment should be done. We agreed on the price and they planned to start in the middle of December, and it would be completed on March 15, 2002. We opened a bank account. We put my twin sister on the account with our names, so she could pay the bills.

Don and I came back to America. We decided we would sell our house in April. I knew it wouldn't be a problem to sell the house since we had made it so beautiful. Knowing the contractors, we gave it an extra month for the apartment to be completed. Before we came home, in Budapest, we purchased all of the new furniture which would go into our new apartment. It just needed to be delivered to the finished apartment.

On the telephone, I asked my twin sister how our apartment was coming along. She said they were not ready. Since we were in the middle of April, I asked her how much work there was still left to do. She was afraid to say it.

"Please tell me, it is very important. That is how we have to plan our house sale and make our moving arrangements."

Our house was sold on the first day we put it on the market. We had to move out quickly, just like it happened to me before. Otherwise, we would have waited there in the house until our apartment was finished. Our house was very beautiful; therefore, several people wanted it on the same day. We had a woman who was crying because she was late putting a contract on the house and she wanted the house so bad.

In two days, we would be leaving for Hungary and our new home. It was midnight, and I couldn't fall asleep. I was worried about how Don would adjust to the Hungarian living. Would he learn the Hungarian language? He did promise he would, but I was still worried. In our beautiful Hungarian language, we can express our love toward each other with so many words. And our songs, the violins . . . no wonder men cry over it. I was afraid that those who were not born in Hungary wouldn't be able to learn and appreciate that language.

Chapter 42

April 2002: We Moved to Hungary

In April 2002, Don received his immigration documents. We got a letter from the Dunaujvaros mayor. They would gladly welcome us into Dunaujvaros. I had to admit we were living very exciting days. We were saying goodbye to America. Laszlo, Victoria, Jerritt, and Jessica would come to visit. Don still was not on talking terms with his three children. I didn't understand it. I didn't see a real reason, but it was their decision. They would receive punishment for abandoning their father.

I remember my first husband told a story to our children. There was a family. The man's father lived with them. Since he was old and sick, his hands shook. His son decided he would carve a wooden bowl and spoon for his father before he broke the ceramic bowl. Then he set his father away from the table, in the corner on a stool. The next day, he saw his little boy carving feverishly. He asked his little boy. "What are you carving, son?" He said, "A wooden bowl, Father. It should be ready by the time you get old." The father recognized the situation, right away. He took the wood and the knife out of his little boy's hand. "It will not be needed, son." Then he went to the corner and helped his father up and set him back at the table. He put the ceramic bowl back in front of him. His little son sat opposite his grandfather and happily smiled at him.

We arrived in Dunaujvaros, and stayed with my twin sister. We were happy to see each other. It was a beautiful springtime. The flowers were blooming. The bushes were just loaded with flowers, and the trees were in full bloom, too. People were on the sidewalk. They had fresh bread in their shopping bags. They talked with their friends and acquaintances. A fruit table was set up next to the sidewalk. Fruits, vegetables, tomatoes, peppers, were spread out on the table. The women and men were buying them.

They would prepare them for lunch. It was a sign everywhere the people were enjoying that beautiful spring.

Gizi, Rozsa, Maria, Viki, and Magdi were coming soon. Now everybody was a grown up. I was very happy there were so many of us. Even though our childhood was very hard, it was nice now to have each other.

We went to see our new home. As we entered the building from the bottom floor, a woman stood in front of me. Angrily, she asked why we had to move in there. Of course, then, I didn't understand her outrage. I didn't understand why that strange woman was so angry at me. I told her, "I moved home."

But she had no idea what that meant. I tried once more to move home into my country. A person who was so extremely lucky, who was able to live her life in her own country in one apartment, how could a person like that understand why I was moving home? I would try to forgive her.

We stepped into the elevator. We pushed the button to the third floor. Number 1 apartment. We right away saw a lot of work needed to be done, yet. The contractor was very sorry, but said they had got emergency work someplace else; therefore, they couldn't work on our apartment.

"But please try to finish our apartment."

"Yes, yes, yes," she promised.

My nephew wrote the company a letter and urged them to finish the apartment as soon as possible. They were already four weeks late with the completion of the apartment. I stood in the apartment for hours, hoping they would work on the apartment. We should have moved in by now. We needed to move in.

We were staying with my twin sister. She had invited us. We thought it would be okay since she was alone, but I noticed she was beginning to get impatient. I really didn't know why. She was not caring for us. She didn't cook. Don brought all the groceries home from the store and the farmer's market.

In the meantime, I was at our new apartment, urging our contractor to finish the apartment. She even cried, and then I felt sorry for her. I gave her a hug and asked her not to cry. "It is not personal," I told her, "but we would wish to move in already."

Finally, in the end of May 2002, we were able to move in our new home, after six weeks' delay. They brought our furniture from Budapest. The electrician put up our chandeliers and light fixtures. My twin sister and I unpacked the boxes. My second cousin, Laci, and his wife, Zsoka, also helped. They were good workers and they needed the money, too.

From Budapest, the Domus Furniture Store sent two men to put the furniture together. We were going to sleep in our new home, finally. You know the saying, "Company is just like fish, after three days, it starts smelling." But I didn't realize that included us.

We found out that there would be a meeting for the building residents and the superintendent who took care of the building's business. We introduced ourselves to the rest of the residents. The professor, Rezso, was the only one who was nice to Don and me. In our stairway on the fourth floor, one woman was unusually nasty. She wanted us to tear down the iron grill in front of our door. They had told us that a lot of people get robbed, and we wanted to protect ourselves. We had the contractor build a nice ornamental, wrought iron grill, with a gate which fenced off our short hallway in front of our door. Of course, the permission was given from the rest of the residents so that could be done. Maybe that woman was not home that day when the signatures were collected. I could not imagine why she was so nasty. So I asked her, "What happened in your life, lady, to become so bitter?"

She said to me, "Fifty years of Communism."

I thought, *Is that all?* She didn't have to leave her country. She did not have to leave her parents. She did not have to leave her siblings. She did not have to live as a refugee in other people's countries. My husband would have settled for that. The poor man wasn't even allowed to be buried in his beloved country! I didn't say anything to her. Instead, I started feeling really sorry for her. Poor woman! There was no feeling in her heart toward others. Soon after that, I heard she moved away.

Pretty soon, we got to know our neighbors. Rezso, the professor, introduced Don to his heart specialist, Dr. Patkai. He was a very pleasant man. Also to our house doctor, Dr. Marczis. We liked him a lot too. And to Dr. Tusai, the surgeon. Rezso and his wife, Maria, are our very dear friends, even today.

After we had lived for two months in Dunaujvaros, we met Attila at the auto dealers where we bought our Mondeo Ford automobile. He was a very pleasant young man. He introduced us to Jolan and her husband, Feri. They were a very pleasant couple. We became very good friends with them. They moved home from Detroit. Feri was working for Ford. They were also Hungarians.

Well, I can not say my sisters visited us a lot. My twin sister, Anna, included. But it was very important to us to live close to each other. She had said, "Eight minutes. That is how far we would be from each other, eight minutes." In two months, she came over maybe three times for a half an hour. I don't know what happened. I was sensing something is wrong. I told Don, "I will go to her and find out what is the problem."

When I got to her apartment, I said to her, "I came to find out what is the problem between us."

She told me, "All right, then. Sit down." Then she scolded me for forty minutes. She said, "I am not going to live in your shadow."

I couldn't believe what I was hearing! How could my twin sister think such a thing? Why did she think like that? And I asked her, "What do you mean by that, 'not going to live in my shadow'?" She didn't answer. How come she did not value our friendship?

She accused me of not protecting her from her doctor's suggestion that she should learn about putting makeup on from me. I didn't protect her from what the woman said in the bank. She said it showed that I came from over there where they are braver, since I wore big ear rings. Then she accused me of thinking I was Gina Lollobrigida.

I told her, "I am not guilty of those things. I am not responsible for what other people say. And, I am your sister, Elizabeth."

But she said, "Let's go sit in the kitchen." That is where we liked to sit and talk.

I told her, "I can not go to the kitchen now; I need to go home."

I found myself at home. Right away, Don saw something terrible had happened to me. He was very concerned. He asked me, "What happened?"

I explained to Don, "She turned against me, the one that I love so much. I always am looking at what I can do for her. When she became a widow, I bought a lot of new things for her apartment so she wouldn't have to worry." I had my life's biggest disappointment. Then it wasn't enough.

On the telephone, she said how terrible a person I was. I had to hang up the telephone on her. I couldn't understand. How could she have so much hatred towards me? What happened to my poor twin sister? I knew one thing. I had never hurt her. Someone steered her against me.

I was sick for weeks. We had been living in this apartment for three months. Everything was in its place. Don had three teachers. He started learning the Hungarian language with a lot of enthusiasm. He purchased a lot of books, dictionaries, and writing tablets. Betty came once a week to our house for two hours. Don went to Margit's apartment, also once a week for two hours. I should mention both of these school teachers spoke English very well. The professor, Rezso, came once a week to our apartment for two hours to teach Don Hungarian. That was wonderful. We were very excited to have that kind of help, with such intelligent people teaching Don Hungarian. It is true that the Hungarian language is hard, but Don had all the opportunity with such wonderful helpers to learn Hungarian.

Of course, we would see how the Hungarian language would stick to him. Our neighbors forgot about the loud noise and the dust while our apartment was getting renovated. We were getting to know each other. They started seeing we were just like them. My dear neighbors, Erzsike, Aranka, Edit, Magdi, Anna, a young couple above us, Kristina and her husband, Rozsa on the first floor. I will never forget her. She had a strong voice.

She called me up and asked me to check her blood pressure. She knew I would come. We created a very pleasant neighborly atmosphere. Erzsike came to visit us since our apartment was warmer than hers—or if she were sad about something, she came to us. Some pastry, a cup of hot chocolate, but most of all, she could tell us if she were unhappy about something.

The time went by. I thought, *It is time for my sister and me to make up.* I called her on the telephone. She told me what and how much I owed her, since she had done so much for me to find an apartment. I couldn't believe my ears! She was practically demanding I pay her for how much I owed her.

In the winter time, I fell down on the sidewalk. My neck got further injured. I went to the doctor. She told me, "It is a problem, but they won't be able to give you a new neck." I was suffering emotionally and physically.

Don was not taking the language education seriously. He spent the time telling stories in English to both of his teachers. He also ate the food he prepared. He spent a lot of time in front of the computer. He was missing American food. He, more and more, didn't care about things. We argued a lot. It seemed like a stranger was in our home. I recommended to him to go home. There was no sense to live that way. He told me he was not going. He felt fine here. For two years, most of the time he heard only the Hungarian language, but he didn't understand the language. Obviously, there were unpleasant feelings.

We went to Spain for two weeks. By the end of the trip, the language had started to irritate me. I would not be able to learn it, either. I was thinking of Don. He must feel that way between us.

One of my sisters made an end-of-summer party. The weather turned chilly, so we went into the house. We were about twenty of us. I looked for Don. Since I couldn't find him in the house, I went outside. He was sitting on a bench with a magazine in his hand and the cat next to him. He was reading. In the meantime, my sister and her husband—they are really nice people and they were very kind to us—didn't understand why Don was not eating anything from the wonderful food. Well, I didn't really understand it, either.

The only thing he looked forward to was Betty, the teacher, coming to our house on Thursdays, and Margit. He was not interested in Rezso, since he didn't speak English. It was scary how little he was interested in learning the language. I wondered how that man could want to live there without a language skill. He was not going to admit that it was not a good idea to move to Hungary. I thought he would not admit to it because it was a very big expense to move to here, since we had everything done in a first-class manner.

Chapter 43

Neck Surgery

My sister Rozsa had a neurosurgeon, and she mentioned to him my problem with my neck. He told her I should visit him. I did just that.

He checked my X-rays, and read my surgery records. In front of him on his desk was a big white envelope. He started drawing on it. Then he showed me. He said, "That is how I am going to fix your neck."

I looked at the drawing, which I did not understand. But, I was very happy. He was willing to fix my neck.

Then I told him, "I will let you know what I am not able to handle. Three months with a hard collar, day and night. That is what I had to endure after my surgery in Washington."

He said to me, "Oh, no. Not at all. A soft collar; only for six weeks."

I couldn't believe my luck. He asked, "We could do it in two weeks. Is that okay?"

"Oh, yes, Doctor."

On Sunday afternoon, Don drove me to the hospital, which was in the next town, about forty minutes. The surgery would be the next day.

I woke with a slight headache. But, I felt fine. I already knew I was in good hands. The telephone rang. My daughter called me from America. She was very happy for the good news. She knew how much I had suffered because of the bad surgery. Don and my sisters came and visited in the afternoon.

On Tuesday, I felt very well, although I could not brag on the food. I waited for Don to come, thinking he would bring me some food. The tap water was pretty bad, too. Don arrived in the late afternoon with empty hands. Oh, well.

On Wednesday, I was really hungry. Don would come and bring me something to eat; I was sure. In late afternoon, Don came empty handed, again.

On Thursday, I was hungry. For supper, we got a piece of bread and a piece of bologna. I looked at the bologna and, whenever I tried to eat it, my stomach got nauseated from it. I was thinking maybe I had outgrown it.

I tried to eat it. I sat in the bed. In one hand, the piece of bread. In my other hand, that round piece of bologna. As I was eating it, I remembered the story about the rich man's dog.

The rich man's dog was very spoiled. The rich man heard that, down at the end of the village, a man lived who was able to cure sick animals. The rich man, with his dog, was on his way to see the man. Maybe he could help to cure his beloved dog. He told the man his dog was not able to eat. "Could you help?" he asked. He would richly reward him. The man looked the dog over and he said to the rich man, "I will try. But you will have to leave him here for three or four days." The rich man saw hope. He agreed to leave his dog with the man. As they were saying goodbye, the man said, "As soon as the dog is well, I will send my son to get you."

As soon as the rich man left the yard, the man locked the dog in a shed. He gave him only water. On the second day, the dog was in the shed. The man looked in on the dog, with a small crabapple in his hand. He threw it to the dog. The dog pushed it aside with his nose. "All right, I will be back tomorrow." Now, it was Wednesday evening. The man looked in on the dog. Again, he threw a crabapple in front of the dog. Now, the dog had not eaten for three days. He was really, really, hungry. That time, he right away ate the crabapple. The man said to his son, "Would you go tell the rich man he can come and pick up his dog tomorrow."

On Thursday, the rich man arrived. The man was already in the yard with the dog on the leash. The rich man anxiously asked. "Is he well, can he eat?" The man took out of his pocket a small crabapple, and he said, "Yes, Sir! He even eats that green crabapple!" And, he threw down the crabapple for the dog. Of course, he right away ate it up. It was more than three days since he had eaten. The rich man was very grateful and paid the man very well.

Let me go back to my story, to the hospital. My doctor was very satisfied with my healing. I thought. *It would be wonderful to take a shower.* As I opened the shower door, from the drainage hole, there was such an awful smell that came up. I right away closed the shower door. I decided I would take a shower at home, since tomorrow was Saturday and I was going home. I told Don "Tomorrow, hurry up and come and take me home."

"Yes, yes," he said.

Finally, it was Saturday. At eleven-thirty, Don was not here. He should have been there already. I was all set. A little nurse took the bandages off my neck. I showed my appreciation to the nurses with money. They hadn't changed my bed all week.

Don was not here, yet. I was ready to go. I would give him ten more minutes. I thought, *If he isn't here, he will be in big trouble. I am so ready to get out of here. It has been such a long week.*

At one-thirty, Don arrived. I asked, "Where have you been? "

He said, "At home."

"But I was waiting for you!"

"Well, I am here!"

At a time like that, it is best not to say anything. Finally, we were on our way. I asked Don to watch the holes on the road. "It is not good for my neck when you go in them."

We would be at the Interspar shortly. Don suggested we go in, since he hadn't done the grocery shopping. I agreed to it, since I was feeling pretty good. Don had the shopping cart, running around in the store like he usually does. What I picked up in my hands, to put in the cart, I had to put down. They were too heavy for my neck. Where was he? Which way did he go? By now, I didn't feel very well. "Oh, here you are." I suggested maybe we should go home so I could lie down.

He said, "There is not much left, I will finish the shopping."

"Then I will sit down somewhere."

Forty minutes later, we were home. Rozsa brought over beef soup and bean casserole. My neighbor, Erzsike, was very happy I was home. After a week, a shower seemed so good!

My twin sister didn't even come to see me. Rather, she was bad-mouthing me to my sisters. And they were just listening. They were afraid of her. They know how well I had treated her through the years. So many of them, and no one would stick up for me. I was very unhappy.

I ran into my sister-in-law on the street. We were happy to see each other. I asked, "Where are you going?"

She said, "I am going home."

I said, "Take me with you."

She said, "Not now."

"All right, then, you come to my apartment."

She said, "Not now, some other time."

"Then tomorrow. You will have time?"

"Okay, I will come tomorrow."

We had a lot to talk about. I always felt sorry for her and her family. My brother, with his drunkenness, caused his family a lot of sorrow. The next day, the bell rang. My sister-in-law was at the door. She stayed long and we had a nice conversation. I think she was lonely, just as I was. She has lived alone since my brother died. It looked like we might be good friends.

She invited us Sunday into her little church in the village. There was a young minister. I loved the way he did the sermon. Every time, I was able to learn something from him. We thought we would come to that little church every Sunday. That is what we did for a while.

All of the sudden, my sister-in-law stopped coming to visit. Sunday, in the church, after the sermon, we used to have coffee and cookies. She was hiding from us. I called her on the telephone. I wanted to find out what the problem was.

She told me, "Nothing, nothing."

I did not get an explanation. She just stayed away without any explanation. We didn't go to that lovely little church after that. We didn't want her to feel uncomfortable. After all, that was her church.

If people would realize they could hurt the other person with their actions, I am sure they would be more careful.

Chapter 44

Vickie, Jerritt, and Jessica Visit Hungary

Easter holiday was coming. My daughter Vickie, and my grandchildren, Jerritt and Jessica, were coming to visit for two weeks. The children got a week's Easter vacation. The school gave them an extra week since they are traveling to Europe. It would be beneficial for their education.

We were very excited. We sent them the plane tickets. Zsa Zsa, my facial lady, told me her neighbor was selling an Easter ham which was very deliciously cured, and I knew my daughter liked that beautiful red meat very much. I ordered a whole ham.

A few days went by, and I looked out of the balcony window. I saw Zsa Zsa getting out of her car. She was carrying something very heavy. I asked her, "Should I come down and help? What are you carrying?"

"Just open the door."

"Hello, what are you carrying?"

She said, "Your ham."

"Really, it is almost bigger than you!" Luckily, we had a big refrigerator. The ham was delicious. Whoever came to our apartment, we gave them a nice big piece.

I asked my fifteen-year-old grandson on the telephone, "What should I cook when you get here?"

He said, "Mama, chicken paprikas."

It had been two years since I saw them last. We were happy to see each other.

We lived one hour from the Budapest Airport. We got home quickly. I heated up the chicken paprikas. "Everyone, wash your hands. Lunch is ready."

My grandson said, "Mama, you even out-did yourself. This chicken paprikas is so delicious."

I asked my daughter why she was crying. "Mother, I missed your cooking so much!"

Don prepared the itinerary. We want to show them so much, so they could see where their mother's roots are, from pretty, little Hungary. We went to see the Parliament. We also saw the round picture which shows the Hungarians coming to Hungary 1100 years ago. Then we went to an ancient, Hungarian horse farm. The Hungarian equivalent of a cowboy showed all of the tricks a horse can do. We also went to Café Gerbeaud's coffee house in Budapest. We saw beautiful Hungarian cities. We wanted to show them everything and more. It was too bad we just had a limited time.

We also visited my little sister, Juliska, in Budapest. We brought a big piece of that wonderful ham to them. Then Kristina, Vickie's cousin, planned a cousin party. When Vickie visited in Hungary, they always made a cousin party, where every cousin showed up, except Lolika. He has no idea what he is missing. What wonderful memories! They proudly showed off their children to each other. When Vickie and the grandchildren go home to America, they take a lot of memories with them.

Don continued his Hungarian education. In the apartment, everything went back to its place. It was quiet there, and lonely.

In the fall of 2004, Don was no longer bothering with the Hungarian learning. The teacher still came, but only English language came out of the room. I had to realize Don was not interested in learning Hungarian. All he would eat is what he cooked.

I brought it up to him. "You don't have to live here, if you don't want to." That is what his behavior was saying.

Finally, he admitted as much. He would not mind if we went back to America. But of course, you can not replant an old tree.

In December, we decided we would go to America, and find out where we could buy a new home. We were going to Florida. That was where Vickie lived. We were going to Virginia, too. That is where we had lived for years. And, my son Laszlo lived there, too. Now we had a new problem. Who were we going to sell that very expensive apartment to? It was not going to be easy.

My daughter was very happy for the news that we were coming.

Chapter 45

We Prepare to Move Back to the USA

Our airplane was filled up with people. Behind us, someone had a very nasty cough. The plane was very cold. And we were so cold. We hoped we were not getting sick. We arrived in Tampa, Florida. The weather was beautiful. Right away, we took off our winter coats. They were not needed here. It was 70 degrees Fahrenheit.

We were going to spend the Christmas in Tampa. The second day we were in America, I noticed that Don was in a very good mood. I continued to watch him. Shortly, I came to the conclusion that it was a good idea to come back to America with Don.

After all, this is his country. And who understands that better than I? You only can be completely happy in your own country.

We heard that in Virginia the houses were very expensive. Maybe we could live in Florida. The weather was very pleasant. Of course, we had no idea how it was in summer time. We had never been in Florida in the summer time, so we didn't know.

We were on our way to find a home. The real estate agent took us to see several older houses. They showed that they had been renovated a few times. We didn't like them. The real estate lady said, "Nearby here, they are building new houses. Would you like to see them?"

We looked at the model houses. There were five different styles we could choose from. They were very pretty. They were building a whole street. We asked, "When will they be ready?" "In six months." "That would be perfect!" We agreed to do the contract. Then we chose what kind of bathtubs, faucets, carpets . . . we chose it all. And the contract was signed. Don was very happy with the whole thing.

Christmas was nice, too. We were at the airport, going to Virginia. We were going to visit my son and our friends. In the morning at the airport, I noticed Don was unusually slow. But then I thought, *Maybe he is just tired.*

We arrived in Washington, and rented a car. We brought our winter coats since it was winter. On the road, we stopped at a little sandwich shop. Don remembered they made good sandwiches there. We bought the sandwiches. Don said, "Yes, they are just like I remembered them." We finished our sandwiches.

We were on our way to Stafford, where Laszlo lived. We were about an hour away from there. Don said he didn't feel the best. We thought he was probably just tired.

It was nice to see my son after two and a half years. The American custom is to take you to a restaurant for dinner. By ten o'clock, we were in our beds in our hotel.

Don was coughing terribly. At midnight, he said, "In the morning we are going to call Laszlo and Marcia. They need to take us to the doctor." I figured we had a problem.

In the morning at eight o'clock, we were at the doctor's office. Don had double pneumonia. The doctor put penicillin into his arm right away. I, myself, got tablets since I was on the borderline with having pneumonia.

We were very satisfied with the Kaiser-Permanente doctor. She took care of us very well. As soon as we felt well, we were going to visit friends.

We went to see the couple who bought our beautiful house. Well, I couldn't believe my eyes! How different our tastes were. I didn't want to come here again. I wanted to remember our beautiful house just the way it was.

Northern Virginia was beautiful. Upscale people live there. In the Pentagon, there are twenty-five thousand people working. Washington and surrounding suburbs were nice, too.

We were getting over with our illness. We decided to try to have lunch at the Red Robin Restaurant the next day. It was a very pleasant place. They have very delicious fish filets and thick French fries.

We went back to Florida. We had one more week there and then back to Dunaujvaros. We were enjoying Florida's 70 degree weather. They had a lot of palm trees and well-taken-care-of yards. With Vickie and her family, we went to the ocean. We enjoyed our remaining time in Florida. The ocean was beautiful. We walked on the edge of the ocean in the beautiful white sand. We also watched a couple of sword swallowers. We bought souvenirs for our Hungarian friends and neighbors.

We were on our way home. I asked my son-in-law, "How long is that bridge?"

He said, "Mama, that is nine kilometers!" We were traveling that Sunshine Skyway Bridge and watching the sun set. It was a big, red, ball going toward the ocean water. We knew that, pretty soon, it was going to fall into the ocean. It was very, very, beautiful. We were watching ahead of us. It seemed like, in front of us, about two hundred cars disappeared into the ocean! It was amazing scenery. We had to watch on the side, too. The sun was going to disappear in a couple of minutes into the ocean. Then it was dark. Only the cars lights gave any light. We leaned back in our seats. We were so very satisfied. What a beautiful day we had! We saw once more God's beautiful present he created for us.

In a half an hour, we were home. Everybody went to bed.

In the morning, I came out of the house. I thought, *I am going to check out the neighborhood.* I looked to my right; I looked to my left. I didn't see a soul anywhere. As I stood there, I tried to figure out what was going on. Where were the people? It seemed like, for some tragic reason, everyone had run away. And they had left these houses here, empty! Right away, I started hoping that where we were going to live it would not be that way.

My daughter showed me the grocery shopping store. There were only old people in it. I asked her, "Vickie, where are the young people and the children?"

She said, "There are not many here." She said, "I knew you would not like that."

Well, I thought, *we already bought the house. There is no sense worrying about it. That is America. Every one is in a car because of the distance. But, you know, I just came from Europe where there are sidewalk cafes, and there are people on the sidewalks. That is what I am used to.*

On January 6, 2005, we arrived in Budapest. The weather was very pleasant. Laci, my second cousin, was here at the airport to pick us up. It was nice to come home to our beautiful apartment. It also was beautiful with the people coming and going on the wide sidewalk. It showed the city's heart was beating. The people stopped with their acquaintances and talked. If we would imagine for a second, how would that city look if the people would disappear from the sidewalks? It would be an ugly, deserted city. We don't even notice that, for over fifty years, these buildings have not been painted. But, if I had to choose people on the sidewalks and in the parks, or paint on the buildings, I would choose the people.

I am unusually attracted to people. But, at the same time, I am very angry at those who are making this beautiful world ugly. For example, I was watching the TV and they were showing the terrorists in Bombay, India. The cowardly terrorists were robbing the innocent people's lives. I sincerely admit that I look into the future with a lot of fear, especially when I see all of those hungry people all over the world. And, it doesn't look like the problem will be solved. Every year, there are more starving grown ups and children.

There was a young man in England, a musician, who was working very hard to wipe out starvation. He gave a lot of concerts, made a lot of money, to help those who are going hungry. Thirty years later, they examined the fruit of his work. When I saw him on TV, I remembered him as a twenty-something young man, filled up with hope and energy. He was going to get rid of the hunger from children's eyes and faces, and the grown ups. Now, there he stood, a gray haired, tired, man. The number of hungry people has multiplied many times. It was a sad sight. Now I feel sorrier for him more than the hungry people.

In January 2005, we called a real estate man, Zsolt. He was a very pleasant young man. We made a deal with him. If he sold our apartment, we would give him our big TV, which was ninety centimeters. Zsolt looked at the TV like it already belonged to him. We knew he was going to work hard to sell our apartment.

By the end of April, we still didn't have a buyer for our apartment. The moving company recommended against our taking our automobile to America. They said we should sell it and buy a new one in Florida. I didn't want to agree to that. I wanted to take it with us. Our car was beautiful and comfortable. It cost nine million forint. But, Don convinced me to sell our automobile. He parts from things easier than I do. Don is lucky, that that is the way I am, otherwise our lives would have gone their separate ways. He is willing to part from anything, except for me. Many times, I brought it up that we were no good for each other, that we should not live together. And he also brought up what I promised when we got married, that we would be together until the end of our lives. He was right; a promise is a promise. We should be very careful in our lives as to what we are promising.

From the next building, a man came to buy our car. Don was worried that maybe no one would be able to buy our apartment. It seemed like he was ready to go home to America. Mr. Kovacs, from the moving company, came from Budapest. He looked around in the apartment. Then he asked what were planned to take with us. We told him, "Everything." He gave us a price for moving and, when the apartment sold, we were to inform him of the moving day.

In the beginning of May, there were beautiful flowers everywhere and new green grass, the way it was three years ago when we came, with so many hopes and dreams. After all, I was going to live at home. I could not have imagined how sad my life would be here. This shows it is not up to us. Other people's actions dictate our happiness.

Zsolt called. He was going to bring a buyer for our apartment. They loved our apartment. We agreed on the price. We sold it for a ten million forint loss. June 22, 2005, was the day we would move. The deal was, one day was for packing, and I would have a day for saying our goodbyes. On June 24, the packing people were still there. I couldn't go to say my goodbyes. My neighbors didn't wait any longer. They came with their presents to say goodbye to us. We cried; it was very emotional. We were going to miss them a lot. They would miss us, too. My sisters came, too. Since I couldn't go to them, I was very worried I would not be able to say goodbye to them.

Early the next morning, we would go to the airport. If my sisters had not come, I wouldn't have been able to say goodbye to them. That would have made me very unhappy. At six at night, the movers finally left with the last box. In an hour, we had to turn over the apartment keys to the new owners. I still had to finish the cleaning. I was already very tired. We didn't even have time to eat. Luckily, Rozsa brought some biscuits for our trip.

The new owner arrived to receive the keys and look over the apartment. While I was showing the apartment to the mother, the big teen-aged kid ate all of our biscuits in the kitchen! I wasn't happy about it. After we turned the apartment over, we went to have dinner. Since I had been standing around all day and cleaning, one of my feet was swollen. It was hard for me to walk. Our hotel was at the end of the Steel Mill Street, but we called a taxi.

Chapter 46

June 25, 2005: We Moved Back to the USA

On the morning of June 25, 2005, at five in the morning, Laci, my second cousin, took us to the airport. We had a pleasant surprise. Zsoka, his wife, came with him, too. We stopped at the gas station to buy some coffee. I remembered how amazed I was at how good coffee came out of a machine! Then we said goodbye to Zsoka, and we were on our way to Budapest Airport. I was very sad. I had said goodbye to my little sister Juliska last week. I did not have any hope we would see her again, since she had lung cancer. When she walked us to the door, I looked back. I knew I would never see her again. I also noticed in our age that moving goes with very big stress.

We changed planes in Frankfurt, Germany. In Washington, we had to go through customs. Don did not sleep on the plane. In Washington, we had to get our suitcases. He was so tired that he didn't recognize any of them. We were on the plane again, to Tampa, Florida, our destination. Since we were going to be on the plane for two and a half hours, I asked Don to try to sleep. And that is what he did. When we arrived in Tampa, he was in very good shape.

We got our suitcases, but we don't see my son-in-law anywhere. He was supposed to pick us up. We stood around for one hour, and then decided to take a taxi.

We were going to Vickie's house. We had been on the road approximately twenty hours. When we got to the house, it was quiet. Only a dog was barking in the house. There was no one to let us in. We paid for our taxi. We sat down on our suitcases. We were too tired to stand. We were hoping the man of the house would come home, or my grandson.

Vickie and Jessica had gone to Virginia for Edit's wedding. Edit was, four years ago, my son's wife, a Hungarian girl whom I suspect had married my son to get a green card. As soon as he suspected what she had done, he left her. Victoria's friendship with Edit cost her dearly. Her brother has not spoken to her since.

Vickie said to me on the telephone, "There is the house. You should enjoy yourselves. We will be home in a week."

Oh, it is very uncomfortable sitting on the suitcase. Finally, my son-in-law came home. He said he could not find us at the airport. Like I said before, at times like that, it is best not to say anything. Oh, it is so wonderful to finally be in bed.

As soon as our systems recovered from the trip and the six hour time difference, which usually required a week, then we would go to see our new house. We were very eager to see how our new house looked.

Since we needed an automobile to get anywhere in America, our son-in-law took us to buy a car. We went into the Toyota automobile dealership. I looked around. I thought, *What a pretty, red car. It is comfortable, too. That is exactly what we need.* Don and I decided to buy it. We went home with a Toyota Corolla automobile. My son-in-law was not happy with us, since he decided he was going to take us to at least twenty places to shop around, the way he would have. He repeatedly told Vickie, "They bought the car at the very first dealer!" Well, we thought he would get over it.

We went to see our house. In our new street, all of our houses were standing, but inside, there was a lot of work to be done. It seemed like when a contractor tells you it will be ready in two weeks that means it will be ready in eight weeks! We could not move into our house. Oh, but it would have been so nice if Vickie had been waiting for us at the airport. And she would have been there when we arrived. Of course, she knew six months ahead of time our arrival date. But, she said, "There is the house!"

Vickie and Jessica came home from Virginia. Jessica brought her girl friend with her for her summer vacation. We are talking about two four-teen-year-old girls. Our bedroom was side by side with theirs. Now, Don and I learned something new, for instance, what two fourteen-year-old teenagers do with their nights. Let me write it down. They play music, laugh and giggle, the door is opening and closing, there is whispering, the refrigerator door is banging, and when they forget that grandmother likes to sleep, there is loud TV playing.

One night, I had already told them three times they were too noisy, and we couldn't sleep. The next day in mid-afternoon, when they got up, I asked my granddaughter, "How long is your company going to stay?"

Jessica said, "Four weeks, Mama. Then, my other is coming."

I asked her, "Other what?"

"Ami, my other girl friend."

"And how old is she?"

"She is thirteen years old."

They promised our container from Hungary would arrive in five weeks. We were going to familiarize ourselves with the new area. But, we always got lost. I didn't understand. Don is a very good navigator. I, on the other hand, would have a hard time to find my way out of a potato sack. One day, I figured it out. I told Don, "I've got it!"

"What did you get?"

"Why we are getting lost. With all of these flat houses, there is nothing to compare in the distance for getting your bearings."

He agreed to it.

We had been in Florida for three weeks and we hadn't slept one good night, yet. Since we had nothing else to do, we went shopping. We needed a TV. We had a very big living room. We would buy a big couch for the middle. We saw the couch in the furniture store. There was a beautiful, big, red couch. It was so big that seven people could be seated on it. Two persons and a child could sleep on it comfortably. Thank God, we didn't have any children! In three days, they would deliver our couch. We decided we were going to sleep on it in our new house. Jessica's constant party was just too much for us.

Chapter 47

We Moved Into Our New American Home

Our new street was filled up with construction vehicles. The new house owners were standing on the sidewalks in the front of their houses. We were getting to know each other. Everyone had a lot of grievances over what the contractor did not do right. The contractor reassured everybody, "There is no need to worry! Everyone will be satisfied." Everybody was hoping so.

The container arrived from Miami. Three men came with a huge moving truck. Our moving contract stated they would put the furniture together, empty the boxes, and put everything where it belonged. They wanted to throw everything down in the garage and leave, since they had to take the big truck back to Miami by that night. So, they had a long way to go from Sun City Center. We showed them the contract. They did put the two beds together, the boxes on the garage floor, and they were on their way. Out of the three men, only one spoke English. So many people live in America for so many years and they do not bother to learn English!

Since we needed a vacuum cleaner, we were on our way to the shopping center. We arrived in forty minutes. As we got out of the car, wow! We never had such an experience! The sun was unbearable! It was shining, and at least 100 degrees Fahrenheit. Right away, we went into the nearest store. We bought ourselves straw hats. So that is how Florida summer is? I really didn't like that! We came out of the store. We sat in the car. It was 105 degrees in the car! I said to Don, "That is not a joke! It is too dangerous!"

He reassured me, "As soon as we are on our way, the car will cool down."

We were on the road to home, and it started raining! The windshield wiper was going as fast as it could, but it couldn't get rid of all of that water from the windshield. We followed the car in front of us. The red tail lights showed us we were still on the road. It was amazing how fast it came. In a half hour, the sun was shining. The next day, we found out that every day about three o'clock in the afternoon it rains that way. Therefore, the grass gets watered every day. We wouldn't need to spend money watering the grass.

In January 2006, my son came from Virginia to visit us. He saw the garage was filled up with boxes. He went to the store and purchased shelves and put all of the boxes on them. And, by the next day, we were able to put the car into the garage. We were very grateful to my son. Like I said before, the car got extremely hot when it was left outside.

Since my son liked baked duck, that is what I made for dinner, with mashed potatoes, and cucumber salad. After four days, he said goodbye to us. We were sorry to see him leaving. He promised he would return next year.

In March 2006, my hip was hurting a lot. It was hard to sleep with it. The doctor said, after X-raying, "You need a hip replacement and if you need any dental work done, that should be done before the hip surgery."

Since we were new in Florida, we went to a dentist we didn't know. When he got through with me, I had un-necessarily lost all of my lower teeth. With his lack of knowledge, he was not able to provide me with a proper denture. Therefore, we had to go to someone else. That one had personality issues. We had to go someplace else. There, I got four mini-dental implants and a very uncomfortable denture.

On July 30, 2006, I had a hip replacement. After the surgery, I regained consciousness a few minutes a day. Finally, seven days after the surgery I was fully awake. I finally knew where I was. For the next two months, I had a horrible headache. Eight weeks after the surgery, the X-ray looked good, but I could not walk. The doctor said that two of my leg muscles had atrophied, in other words, died. That is why I could not walk.

Seven months later, the doctor opened up my thigh. After six weeks, I realized there was no improvement. I asked the doctor what he had found during the second surgery. I told him I had two questions for him. What can I expect? And, what had he found?

It was lucky Don and I were sitting on the chair. From our surprise, we would have fallen on the ground. We had never seen such huge arrogance in a doctor like he demonstrated. He said to me, "Stop talking and listen!"

I motioned that I was listening.

He proceeded to say, "I didn't find anything, and I don't know what you can expect." Then he was done with me. That was what happened to me in Florida, but other people in the street, they all have horror stories, too.

It is now 2007. I am waiting to get well enough to go to my Hungarian dentist to get a proper denture. My days are nothing but suffering with the bad denture and the bad hip replacement.

Chapter 48

2007: Roots

Since I was house bound for so long, my new neighbors found their friends and I found myself alone. I heard there would be a fashion show in one of our clubs. I decided to go to it. A hostess took me into the room. She asked me who I came with. I told her I came alone. There was a little table next to the wall and she seated me there. Pretty soon, the whole room filled up. In the room were approximately eighty women, sitting at long tables. Some were seated at round tables. They started ordering their lunch. Since I didn't know there would be lunch, I had eaten at home. I ordered a Coca-Cola. When the lunch was served to everyone, the fashion show started. The models walked around the room. They showed their over-decorated sequined blouses. That lasted about an hour and a half. I came to the conclusion they did not have one piece of an elegant wardrobe.

I really needed to renew my wardrobe, since I had grown out of my clothes. I was sitting alone. I looked at all of these women. They were from the Red Hat Society, my neighbors from our street, and then myself, alone at a small table next to the wall. Since I don't have a pushy personality, I wished someone or somebody would invite me to their table. It was very uncomfortable sitting all by myself. I felt like when a child is put in a corner to be punished. But, it was just a wish.

There was no one who would care, out of so many. All these people were thinking how generous they were towards other human beings. Oh, they gladly donated their unwanted stuff, but it was very rare to find those who really care. That is how it was at that fashion show.

I feel this story fits in right after my fashion show experience. I talked about one of my sisters who also lives in America. It was her husband's desire to come to America with their three-month-old baby. So, they immigrated into the United States. After her divorce, she didn't find herself. She moved back to Hungary to be with her sisters and the other relatives that she grew up with. She thought it would be good to live there. After a short while, she didn't find herself there, either. She moved back to America. After a short while again, she felt she would be happier in Hungary. Well, she moved there, again. She still didn't find herself, so she came back. Now, she lives in America. We should feel sorry for her, shouldn't we? We cannot just say she is crazy, and that is that.

I, myself, feel very sorry for her. One day I was talking to one of my sisters on the telephone. I was asking her how our sister was since I was not in a talking relationship with her. Between us are a lot of years, and I wasn't there when she was growing up. It really hit my ear when my sister said, "I wrote her a letter, a nice letter. I wrote it nicely. She should find herself in America, since she has no roots here."

I was thinking, *Where are her roots, if not at home where she grew up?* I wondered how our sister who wrote the nice letter would feel if, one day, her sisters, the relatives she sees often, acquaintances she talks to daily, and the people from the sidewalks, if one day they all disappeared. I am sure she would feel like our sister who lives in America. I am sure she would try to get all of that back, no matter what the price.

But she can't. In the end, we don't belong anywhere.

A Hungarian movie star was being interviewed. She was asked. "Where are you the happiest?" She replied, "On an airplane heading home." So, they say our roots are here. Then they say our roots are over there. It is no wonder so many of us are not able to find ourselves.

In July 2007, we went to Hungary to visit the relatives. We were also going to Sopron to see the wonderful dentist we know. Rozsa and the girls rented us a furnished apartment. In the apartment, it had everything that was needed. It was nice to see the relatives and our friends. Then we had very good luck with our dentist, too. My life would be so much better, since I received a proper denture.

Chapter 49

2007: I Am Going to Write This Book

In December, Vickie's mother-in-law visited from Virginia. Barbara, Vickie, and I, the three of us, went to the ocean to find some sharks' teeth in the ocean sand. During lunch, I started telling one of my stories. Barbara said, "You should write a book out of your life stories because they are so very interesting."

I told her I didn't have anyone to help me.

She right away said, "I will help you."

I was very happy for the offer. We decided I would come to Virginia to visit her in June 2008.

She lived alone in Virginia with her two little doggies. It was a quiet place. We wouldn't be disturbed and we would begin writing the book! We planned it out. I would talk on a cassette tape and she would type it. I bought a tape recorder and lots of cassettes.

Barbara and I sat at the kitchen table. The tape recorder was all set up, and the cassette was going around. Barbara said, "Now tell the story!"

"Where should I begin? After all, we are going to write my life's story down here." I started talking in the way it came into my mind. In the end, we would put the stories in the right sequence.

One week passed. That recording machine was staring at me. Barbara was urging me, "Go ahead, tell the story. Say it!"

I felt I was under terrible stress. I felt my blood pressure go way up. After I had been there for ten days, I couldn't get away from the thought, *Ten days! And my son has not come to see me!*

On the telephone, he said he was busy. We saw each other a year and a half ago the last time.

On Saturday, finally, my son was able to see me. Barbara dropped me off at his home. She would leave me with my son until Wednesday. A year and a half was a long time ago. I miss my forty-eight-year-old son.

I said to myself, *I am going to enjoy that visit.*

His townhouse neighbors probably came from at least five countries. For the next two days, there would be parties. My son and his girlfriend were taking me to these parties, since the custom is to show up at each party. My son asked me, "You don't mind, do you, Mother?"

On Monday, Marcia, the lady of the house, went to work. My son stayed home three days to be with me. Monday, he took me to see my friends, Trudi and Mooney. Tuesday, he showed me the new shopping center. Then, Wednesday, he was supposed to take me back to Barbara's.

My son took me back to Barbara's house. I still had eight days in Virginia. I called my wonderful neighbor of many years. She was very happy to find out that I was in Virginia. Judy, right away, came and picked me up. We had a wonderful time together. We reminisced about when we were young and raising our children.

I visited my dear friend Esther, also. I was planning to spend three days with her. I thought we had a lot to catch up, although I frequently called her on the telephone to see if she were all right. But, my three days with Esther were very stressful. She was not in a friendly mood. So, I was glad to say goodbye to her.

Back in Barbara's house, we continued the book writing. On the table was the recording machine. As soon as I looked at the machine, I felt the stress. The machine was saying, "Tell me! Tell me!" I realized Barbara and I were not going to write that book that way.

The day I was to leave Virginia. I said goodbye to everyone. It had been eight days since my son brought me back to Barbara's. I decided to call him on the telephone and to say goodbye. My son said, "I will come to the airport with you." I was very happy for the offer.

I spent a month in Virginia. I haven't talked to my friend Esther since. I didn't forgive her yet. I needed a friend and she was not there for me. I will forgive her, later. With Barbara, we became best friends. Judy was very sweet and kind. Trudi, Mooney, Lila, Istvan, Judith; they were very happy we were able to see each other again.

Don told me every day what was happening in Florida. He said, "I am waiting for you." And he did, with twelve red roses at the airport. I will be honest, I was mad at Don when I left. I needed good friends. Now, I am home and it is good to sleep in my bed.

I decided that, when I got home, I would get a paper and pen in my hands and begin at the beginning, in Hungarian. Then I thought, *The Hungarian reader will understand these stories, anyway.* But, it would be appreciated if everyone knew what a refugee and immigrant goes through. Now I have four hundred handwritten pages. I thought I had better find a Hungarian who would type it for me. I told of my interest at the Hungarian Club. I let everyone know what I was looking for. Then I found Szabolcs, who was visiting his mother in Florida.

Szabolcs agreed to do the typing for me. I think my guardian angel had a hand in this.

Chapter 50

2008: I Returned to Florida

I am very happy Don and I purchased a condo/apartment and we are moving back to beautiful Virginia where we lived many years. When we were visiting last month, I came to the conclusion that is the place where I feel at home.

I have to write down how the Hungarians keep in touch. On December 13, 2008, an invitation came. The invitation said, "All Hungarians are invited to Plant City to the Hungarian Club where we are nurturing our Hungarian culture and heritage." Then there was a menu of chicken soup, baked sausage, mashed potatoes, and red cabbage. Before lunch, we sang, *God Bless America.* After that, we sang the Hungarian anthem, *God Bless the Hungarians.* Then we sang the Transylvanian anthem which says, "Who knows where the end is? Where is the troubled road taking us?"

The area Hungarians gladly showed up in their club. They number about one hundred. Their ages are between sixty and ninety. It does not look like after we die there will be anyone to take our places which the 1956 Hungarians started to keep their country's memories alive and to have a place where they were able to see their fellow countrymen.

The newcomers are not finding it important to cherish their inheritance. It is a big loss for Hungary, but it is a bigger loss to our young Hungarians. It is true that our country suffered a lot. It was invaded many, many times. Yet, she had many smart people born there. When I was asked where I am from, I proudly said, "I am a Hungarian!"

A lot of events happen in one's life. I wrote sixty-seven years of memories into this book. I have come to the end of my book. I relived many sweet memories, but also many, many, sad ones. My tears have fallen a lot. My life suffered a lot of loss the past seventy-two years, but if we can cherish our love in our heart, and if we were able to hand our hands to one person, then we can not say our lives were wasted.

A Hungarian Woman's Life—who loved her country, and her fellow man.

Erzsebet Kertesz Dobosi Croll